GARDENING

in

OMA

and

the UAE

written and photographed

by

Anne Love

Happy Birthday Do love annie

Personal Acknowledgments

It is with great pleasure that I would like to acknowledge the following individuals whose professional horticultural and other expertise has contributed greatly to the content of this book.

Ali Al Abdullatif, Director www.GardeningWorldOman.com Chairman of Horticultural Association of Oman.

Gurmeet R. Bains, Abu Imad for Agricultural Products Seeb, Oman.

Valerie Charmers, Vice Chairman Dubai Natural History Group, part of the Emirates Natural History Group www.enhg.org

Shahina Ghazanfar, Royal Botanic Gardens Kew, UK.

Maggie Jeans M.Ed. Director www.almanahil-books.com

Sunil Lobo, Landscape Manager W J Towell & CO. (LLC) Oman

Matt Reynolds, Senior Landscape Architect, Middle East & India, Atkins, Muscat.

Mir Mohammed Ali Khan, expert nurseryman.

Dr. Annette Patzelt of the Oman Botanic Garden

Clive Winbow, author of The Native Plants of Oman. An introduction.

William Wilks for the invertebrate photographs.

My husband Charlie for his calm firm encouragement and patience.
Friends Denise Broadfoot, Cassandra Bullock, Anne Parker.
To all the garden owners who I have accosted to let a stranger photograph their gardens, a very warm thanks, their generosity and hospitality has been outstanding.

Anne Love

A note on plant names

Plant names are continually changing. I have done my best to ensure that the names are correct and up to date by checking several different sources and in some cases sending plant material to the Royal Botanic Gardens at Kew, UK. Where an older name is in common use in the region I have noted the synonym or mentioned this in the text. I hope any inaccuracies do not detract from your enjoyment of the book.

CONTENTS

September 2009

January 2010

INTRODUCTION

Whether your aim is colourful pots of annuals over the winter or a garden full of trees and shrubs, this is a 'hands on' guide to help people garden more successfully in the region. The hot dry conditions make the cool green of plants very much appreciated and the look of any outdoor space can be dramatically enhanced with just a few plants.

The growing season in the region is long and there is always something in flower. The rate of growth of many plants is astonishing, annual and permanent climbers can cover harsh concrete walls in months, while shrubs and trees can be a substantial size within a year. There is an extensive range of plants available at modest prices from nurseries throughout the region. Details of the locations of the main centres are listed in the appendix.

Native flora is ideally suited to the environment and benefits the wider ecosystem being host to native insects and birds. Native plants are not yet widely available in the nurseries but the species mentioned in the book are easy to grow from seed. They want to grow here and need no coaxing. Once established native plants need very little water to thrive and are a long term contribution to the environment. The establishment of the Oman Botanic Garden will undoubtedly provide information on growing many more natives for landscapers and gardeners alike.

Oman and the UAE is an exciting and rewarding region for gardeners. Don't let the heat deter you.

April 2009

December 2009

Climate

The majority of Oman and the UAE has an extremely hot and arid climate. Most of the population live on the coastal plains of the region where rainfall is below 20 ml a year. Average summer (May/June–October) temperatures are 33-35°C (91.4-95°F) but the maximum temperatures are considerably higher with temperatures frequently in the high forties with occasional spikes of over 50°C. Temperatures in Oman are reduced significantly due to the influence of the Indian Monsoon.

Winter temperatures (October–April) are pleasant and the main growing and flowering time for many plants. Minimum average temperatures are 15-18°C (59-64.4°F) and maximum average temperatures 26-27°C (78.8-80.6°F). Mountain areas can be cold and receive significant rainfall .

The climate naturally supports xerophytic, drought tolerant, shrubs and grasses, with some small areas of dry tropical scrub and thorn forest. To grow plants from wetter areas additional water is essential.

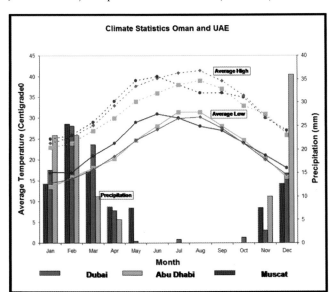

Commercial and home-made compost bins

Bev Mann

In temperate regions soil is produced by rain, frost, plants and micro organisms breaking down the rocks to fine particles and combining with organic material from decaying vegetation. In arid regions such as Oman and the UAE this process is very slow, producing minimal natural soil and even smaller amounts of organic material. In addition, much of the bed rock of the region is limestone which produces alkaline soils inhibiting plant growth. In some areas salinity may also be a problem. As the traditional farming terraces and modern parks of the region admirably demonstrate these problems can be overcome to produce wonderful green oases.

Depending on what exists on the original site additional material will usually need to be brought in to improve the quality and depth of soil. Even established gardens will benefit from additional organic material.

Before ordering soil materials it is helpful to have a basic idea of what soil types are present and what are the desirable soil conditions for plant growth.

Soil types found in the region

Sandy soils

Where there is any depth of natural material this is most commonly sand. Sand is made up of large particles that are easy to work and well drained which many plants require, especially at humid times of the year when plants can be prone to rot. The disadvantage of sand is that it contains no nutrients and any that are added are washed away rapidly. Sandy soils dry out very quickly, heat up fast and also require constant irrigation and feeding for plants to thrive.

Fine silty soils

These types of soils are usually brought in from wadi basins and recharge dams and commonly sold as 'wadi soil'. They are made up of very fine particles which form a solid mass and hold water tenaciously. With excess water the silt becomes a slimy mud and when it dries it forms lumps as hard as bricks. Though similar to clay when wet it doesn't mould or hold its shape. Silt has little or no air spaces making it a hostile environment for roots as they need air for respiration. Water can not penetrate the dense material so that the surface may have pools of water lying on it while underneath it remains dry. Green alga often forms on the surface because of the poor drainage.

Neither silt or sand is ideal but a mix of the two making a loamy soil makes a good medium for plant growth. The mix of particle size holds water better than sand while allowing better aeration and drainage than silt.

Essential organic material

Organic material comes in many forms; peat, compost, tree bark, coconut fiber, animal manure or home made compost. Organic material acts in three ways;

1. As a soil conditioner, increasing moisture retention without water logging.

2. It contains beneficial soil bacteria which break down micro-nutrients into simple forms which plants can absorb that are essential for plant growth.

3. It is essentially acidic and counteracts the generally high alkaline levels of soils in the region.

Some organic material such as animal manure both condition and add nutrients to the soil. Peat, on the other hand, is a good conditioner but is very low in nutrients. Organic material is broken down by soil bacteria very quickly in high temperatures. In six months to a year all the organic material will have been broken down and used. Organic material needs to be regularly added to the soil. Loosen the surface soil and dig in the organic material into the moisture zone of the irrigation. Some of the surface roots will be destroyed but they will be quickly replaced.

Vermiculite and Perlite

These are inorganic artificial chips and look like brilliant white fine gravel often seen in imported pot plant soil. Vermiculite (lightweight expanded mica) or Perlite (porous volcanic rock) are both good additions to soil. They are featherweight, clean and cheaper by volume than peat. Both hold many times their weight in water and unlike peat they are easy to re-wet. Their granular form adds valuable air spaces to the mix and helps reduce soil compaction. They are especially useful for containers and cuttings. Being inorganic they remain permanently in the soil and improve the structure but contain no plant food.

Soil mixes used by landscapers

The following soil mixes are used by landscapers in the region. They are approximate percentages and vary with what is locally available and how coarse or fine the material is. If the sand is very fine less wadi soil will be needed otherwise the drainage will be poor. The more organic material the better.

Sand	Other materials
80%	20% organic material
80%	10% organic material and 10% inorganic chips
50%	20% organic material and 30% wadi soil

Soil problems

Problems associated commonly with regional soils are alkalinity, salinity and a hardpan layer.

Soil Alkalinity

Acidity or alkalinity is measured on a pH scale from 0 - 14. Above 7 the soil is alkaline, below 6.5 it is said to be acid. The ideal level of soil pH for plant growth is between 6.5 to 7, neutral to slightly acid. Soil pH is influenced by the base rock, which over much of the region is dominated by limestone and soils tend to be alkaline. The problem with high levels of alkalinity is that it prevents plants taking up vital nutrients from the soil, mainly iron and magnesium, which leads to poor growth and a condition called chlorosis. Symptoms of chlorosis are that the mid-ribs and veins are dark green while the rest of the leaf is pale. This can be overcome in two ways; by adding organic material which increases soil acidity, or, by using specially prepared fertilizers which contain essential iron, copper, magnesium and zinc in fast acting 'chelated' or 'sequestered' forms. These are absorbed quickly through roots and leaves. They also lower the soil pH (increases soil acidity) so the plants are able to absorb the existing nutrients more readily.

Soil Salinity

Salts occur naturally in all soils. Where there is sufficient rainfall the salts are dissolved and washed away into streams and the sea. In arid areas or where there is no quick route to the sea, some of this water evaporates and the dissolved salts become more concentrated. In arid areas this can result in the formation of salt lakes or in brackish ground water, salinized soil, or salt deposits. Soil salinity is usually measured and expressed in terms of total dissolved solids (TDS) or electrical conductivity (EC).

E.C. (µS/cm)	T.D.S. (mg/l)	Salinity	Problems with ornamental plants
2,000	1,500	Drinking water	None
2,000 - 6,000	1,500 - 4,000	Low	Occasional
6,000 - 10,000	4,000 - 6,500	Medium	Moderately common
10,000 - 16,000	6,500 - 10,000	High	Frequent
> 16,000	> 10,000	Very High	Universal
50,000 Sea water	35,000 Sea water		

Effects of salinity

Salinity generally reduces plant growth. Plants fail to thrive often producing small pale leaves and in extreme cases the leaf edges brown and the plant dies. Often the plant continues to exist but is always a poor specimen. If plants show signs of poor growth despite regular applications of fertilizer have the soil tested.

Salts can be leached out by abundant application of fresh water in sites where the drainage is good. Bringing in sweet soil and growing plants in free-draining raised beds is also a possibility. Long term, however, problems with salinity often re-occur. Better by far to grow tougher, more salt tolerant plants, of which there is an extensive range, and grow sensitive plants in containers. General levels of salt tolerance are given in the plant descriptions. For specific figures see the tables at the back of the book.

Hardpan layer

A hardpan is a layer of hard impermeable dense material, usually the result of a coagulation of minerals and soil found below the soil surface. The hardpan prevents water draining through it which causes localized water logging and is a barrier to plant roots. It can usually be broken up manually with a pick axe and the addition of organic material helps prevent its reoccurrence.

Fertilizers and the mysteries of NPK

Plant Nutrients

The most important nutrients for plant growth which are required regularly in relatively large quantities are:

Nitrogen (N): promotes vigorous leafy growth.
Phosphorus (P): assists strong root growth.
Potassium (K): improves flowering, fruiting and aids disease and drought resistance.

These elements are the key components of most fertilizers and are always written as NPK. To remember which element does what memorize the rhyme 'Up down and all around'

Chemical fertilizer is often referred to simply as NPK and the ratio of these three elements is written 20-10-20, meaning that this product contains 20% nitrogen, 10% phosphorous and 20% potassium, the rest is filler.

Plants also require 'minor' or 'trace' elements such as iron, manganese, boron, molybdenum, zinc and copper. Plants lacking any of these elements show various conditions. The most common are:

Deficient element	Symptom
Nitrogen (N)	Slow stunted growth and pale leaves
Phosphorus (P)	Stunted growth and red or purple leaves
Potassium (K)	Pale yellow or brown leaves
Magnesium (Mg)	Yellowing of older leaves
Iron (Fe)	Yellowing of young leaves
Iron/magnesium (Fe/Mg)	Yellowing leaves between dark veins, known as 'chlorosis'

chlorosis

Buying and using Fertilizers

In the regional conditions plant growth is rapid, soils are often sandy and free-draining allowing the nutrients to wash away, so fertilizers constantly need replenishing. What you use depends on the size of your garden and your enthusiasm. The golden rule is: 'A Little and Often'. Small applications of fertilizer regularly are infinitely better than one big lot.

Agricultural NPK

The cheapest fertilizers are large sacks of NPK often sold loose by nurseries in handy kilo bags. It is usually in the form of water soluble granules. The ratio of Nitrogen, Phosphorus and Potassium is written on the sack, check with the supplier what it is. These are really intended for agricultural purposes and rates of application are in kilos per square hectare. The higher the numbers, 15-15-15, the stronger it is. For the home gardener, a 15 ml table spoonful per established plant scattered round the root zone every two months during the growing season will be sufficient. Rake it into the soil and water well. Alternatively dissolve a 10 ml desert spoonful in a 10 litre watering can and water round the plants.

Fertilizer of this type is very strong, don't be tempted to add 'a bit more', over-application can burn plants, defoliating them completely and possibly killing them. If in doubt always use less than you think you need. The only remedy if you used too much fertilizer is to water copiously to try and wash out the fertilizer. By the time you see the signs, however, the damage has already been done. Agricultural fertilizer is not suitable for seedlings or pot plants. If you only use this type of fertilizer you will need to apply micro-nutrients separately. *See below.*

Complete Soluble Fertilizers

A granular powder containing NPK plus a range of micro-nutrients, Magnesium, Manganese, Iron, Sulphur and minute quantities of Zinc, Calcium, Boron. Rates of application are detailed on the packet according to the type of plant. The solution is watered into the soils and can also be watered over the leaves as a foliage feed but never in direct sunshine. These are designed for garden use and can be used for established plants, pot plants, seedlings and indoor plants. Phostrogen™ and Osmocote™ are two well known makes with a wide range of products and packet sizes, often available in supermarkets. Relatively expensive but very convenient and simple to use.

Complete Slow Release Fertilizers

These dissolve slowly into the soil and usually one application is sufficient for the growing season. Their make up varies with the manufacturer, all will contain NPK and some micro-nutrients. They are most effective mixed into the soil so are great for new plants and annuals. These are the most expensive type but require few applications and minimal effort and give plants constant nutrients.

Micro-nutrients only

These contain no NPK but only trace elements. These are highly concentrated multi-micro-nutrient fertilizers with the emphasis on iron and magnesium to counteract Chlorosois on alkaline limestone soils. Application rates are outlined in great detail, follow them precisely. Packages available in the region are typically intended for agriculture, so rates of application read "dissolve 500 g in 200 lt of water", but it is simple to translate this into 5 g in 2 lt of water. Weigh out the first application then pour the powder into a convenient measure, yoghurt pot or similar and mark the level, keep this in the packet for future use.

Epsom Salts

Epsom salts, available from chemists, can be used to treat magnesium deficiency. Symptoms are inter-veinal chlorosis where the central vein of the leaves stays green but the areas between are yellow. Mix 20 g of Epsom salts in 1 lt of water and spray on as a folia feed. Or add it directly to the soil at 25 g per square metre.

Specialized fertilizers

Tomato fertilizers have a different ratio of NPK, being rich in potassium (K), this is excellent for tomatoes and flowering pot plants. Follow the manufacturers recommendations. It also works on Bougainvillea producing bracts of a more intense colour. Apply after pruning and when the old flowers have faded, approximately every six weeks.

Storage

All fertilizer granules are hygroscopic, that is they attract water and in the humid conditions of the region they soon become rock solid and unusable. Store them in damp proof containers preferably indoors. Large sacks can be stored in a plastic dustbin with a tightly fitting lid.

Organic Fertilizers

Organic fertilizers such as manure will be rich in nitrogen, can be dug in as described above or can be made into a solution. Put 10%, by volume, of manure into a plastic dustbin or similar and fill the container with water. Leave it to stand for several hours then use with caution on established plants and trees only, never on seedlings.

How to make home made compost

Making compost in the Gulf is both quick and simple as one of the essential ingredients is amply available, heat. Forget the metre square heaps needed to generate enough heat for composting in northern Europe, here you can be successful with small quantities in an enclosed container.

The commercially designed compost tumbler bins are ideal but may have to be imported. Alternatively, blue chemical barrels can be converted into tumbler bins.* The horizontal rotation is easier to turn when partly full. The vertical rotation needs to be mostly full so the weight of the material at the bottom is counter-balanced by the material at the top. Alternatively use two identical containers such as dustbins with lids. All containers will need small ventilation holes.

1. Collect organic material to fill the container. A good mixture of material is needed to provide the micro-organisms with sufficient amounts of carbon and nitrogen to work efficiently. Carbon comes from woody material, nitrogen is in fresh green matter. The ratio required is is about 30% woody to 70% green.

2. Woody material can include leaves and twigs but usually it is hard to collect enough to make the right balance. Easiest by far is to collect wood shavings, preferably hardwood, free from the local carpenters shop. Not enough dry woody material and the compost becomes smelly, wet and slimy.

3. Green material includes grass, prunings, spent flowers, plants, vegetables and peelings.

4. Chop up everything as fine as possible and mix it up.

5. The mix needs to be just moist like a wrung out cloth. In the early stages the green material releases moisture as it breaks down so the original material should be on the dry side.

6. Leave the material for two days in the closed container After two days the material will have shrunk considerably and be warm to touch, about 10-20°C above the ambient temperature.

7. Now either tumble the bin daily or pour the material from one container to the other.

8. Small fruit flies will get into the bin but these are killed by turning the material over, otherwise it should be pest free. There will be a mild but not unpleasant smell in the initial stages.

9. After about 10 days grass and leaves are unrecognizable but twigs are still intact and the compost looks coarse and lumpy.

10. By six weeks, the process is complete. The material will be much finer and look more like commercial compost.

Home made compost is an excellent soil conditioner but will probably be low in nutrients so use it together with a complete fertilizer for maximum effect.

*See page 6 for pictures of different types of compost bin

Water in the region is a very precious commodity. Try to conserve water as much as possible by irrigating efficiently. Always irrigate at night to reduce evaporation and avoid surface run off. Maintain watering equipment so water is not wasted through leaks.

Water

Water requirements

How much water is a constant concern to gardeners and even in the hot dry climates of the region probably the majority of gardens are over-watered. Below is a rough guide to the maximum and minimum water requirements during winter and summer.

VEGETATION	MIN - water at 20C requirement litres per day per sq. metre	MAX - water at 40C requirement litres per day per sq. metre
Grass lawns	4	10
Ground cover - *Wedahlia*	3	10
Small bush - *Lantana*	1.5	6
Medium bush - *Ixora*	3	10
Large bush - *Hibiscus*	4	25
Small tree - *Cordia*	10	50
Medium tree - *Delonix*	30	100
Large tree - fruiting date palm	40	120

Irrigation methods

Hand watering

Is best done early morning or at dusk to reduce evaporation and to avoid burning the leaves with drops of water which act like lenses and magnify the effect of the sun. Dig a depression around each shrub which will act as a reservoir for water, allowing it to soak in. To encourage deep rooting of trees, bury a length of plastic water pipe into the soil at the bottom of the newly planted root zone and water through the pipe. The water runs into the soil creating a moisture zone well below the soil surface. Inevitably hand watering is difficult to control, seedlings are washed away while trees tend to be short of water and have a predominance of surface roots. This is also the most wasteful method of watering with high evaporation losses and surface run off. For anything but the smallest garden hand watering is unsatisfactory in the long term.

Drip feed irrigation.

Plastic piping is laid on the soil surface or concealed just underneath and where required the pipe is pierced and fitted with a dripper. The dripper delivers a known quantity per hour. Water consumption is approximately 30% less using drip-feed irrigation, compared to hand watering or flood irrigation.

The system can be attached directly to a tap but it is more usual to use a mechanical or electronic timer together with a solenoid valve which turns the flow on and off. In addition a pressure controller should be added to reduce the mains pressure, allowing the drippers to work correctly and reducing the problem of joints bursting open. Drippers create a moist zone, ideally in the shape of an inverted cone. In reality the area and depth of the moisture zone is dependent on the soil type and the amount and frequency of irrigation. Though there will be some surface evaporation the rate of delivery is so slow that surface run-off is unlikely. The wettest area with drip irrigation is on the surface which encourages masses of surface roots. This can be over come to some extent by regularly leaving the irrigation on for extended periods every 15 days and then not irrigating for two days until the soil surface has really dried out.

Equipment required

Piping and drippers are very easy to install and the saving on water consumption will go a long way to offset the initial cost. The range of accessories is extensive with drippers sizes ranging from 2-22 lt (½ to 5 gallons UK) per hour. Some drippers can be set to deliver different amounts e.g. 0–6 lt per hour. These are very flexible and can be set to deliver more as the plant grows or turned off when not required, for instance on winter herbs and annual beds which are empty in the summer. Fine flexible hose can be attached to drippers to distribute water to small annuals or pots. Check with a main dealer for details of the full range of equipment.

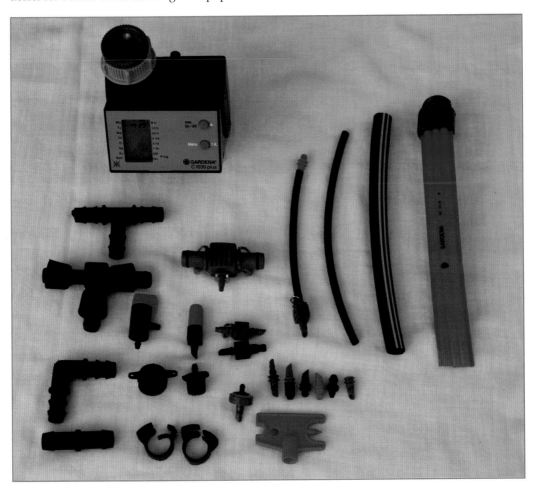

Positioning drippers

Drippers should be placed well away from the trunks of trees and bushes to encourage spreading roots to anchor the plant. For trees and large shrubs it is better to have a circle of small drippers rather than a single large one. As plants grow additional drippers will need to be added and others removed and blocked. Check that drippers are still flowing correctly and replace any that are clogged or letting water gush out. Where possible bury the pipe since it will last longer out of the sunlight and protect it from being walked on. Where leaks do occur cut out the faulty pipe section and use connectors to put in a new section of pipe.

Sprays and sprinklers.

Mainly used for lawn irrigation. They have to be run on a separate pipeline and at a different time from drippers as they require greater pressure to operate.

O ne of the pleasures of gardening is producing new plants yourself. The two main methods are by sowing seeds or taking cuttings.

Seed scarification to aid germination

Most seeds germinate easily given the right conditions of light, temperature and moisture. Some seeds with hard coats need to be scarified to speed up the process. In wild conditions seed lying on the ground would eventually be broken down by the sun, rain, wind and bacteria. Trees seeds can take more than a year for this to happen. Many hard small seeds such as Parsley and Morning Glory need to be soaked for 12-24 hours in warm water. Other seeds require their tough coats to be nicked. **The picture shows Canna seeds after 10 days in warm water**. The ones on the left have had their seed coats nicked, the others not. Place the seed on a rough surface, so its easier to grip and use a sharp blade to just cut through the outer brown coat so the white inside is visible. Other methods include using a file or nail clippers. Then soak in warm water. Many seeds will visibly swell, showing the water has penetrated the seed. Now sow in the normal way.

Sowing seeds

There are three options when sowing seeds: directly into the ground/flowering position; seed trays; peat discs, individual micro pots or root trainers.

Large, tough seeds such as Marigolds, Morning Glory and Zinnias are all intolerant of root disturbance and should be planted directly into the ground/flowering position. Small dust-like seeds like Busy Lizzies can not survive the rigors of direct planting. Grow them in seed trays and pot up into larger containers before planting out. Many other seeds can be individually planted into mini containers, trays of micro pots or peat discs. Peat discs are easiest to keep moist and can be transplanted whole into the flowering position. Root trainers are very deep tubular pots which can be unclipped to allow the plant to be removed with no root disturbance. These are excellent for tree seeds and allowing tap roots to develop properly.

Moringa seedling in a 'Root Trainer'

Direct sowing

Prepare the ground by adding organic material such as peat or home-made compost and digging it well in. Mix fertilizer into the soil and leave for several days, keeping the soil moist before planting. Alternatively liquid fertilizer can be watered in regularly once the seeds have germinated. Sow the seeds thinly in a marked area and sieve a covering of soil over them.

As a rough guide seeds should be covered by soil to a depth of three times their thickness. Check the back of the packet for specific planting instructions. Do not plant the entire packet at once, but save some seeds to fill in the gaps once the seeds have germinated. This will also give staggered flowering times. The seeds must be kept moist, water lightly and frequently and preferably keep the area temporarily shaded. Palm fronds are easy to prop up above a newly planted area.

Once established, thin out the seedlings of larger plants such as Marigolds and Zinnia to the recommended spacing. Others, such as Alyssum and Portulaca are tolerant of crowding and can be left.

Seed trays

Any durable container can be used as a seed tray, though small shallow containers tend to dry out very quickly. The all-purpose potting composts available tend to be unnecessarily rich in nutrients and too soggy for high humidity conditions. Improve drainage and reduce the nutrient content by adding 15% salt-free sand or vermiculite/perlite. Mix well and add enough water to moisten the compost mix. Fill the container with potting compost and sprinkle the seeds sparingly over the surface. Some seeds need light to germinate and these are just pressed into the surface. Others should be covered by sieving dry compost over the container. Use a dedicated kitchen sieve. Water lightly and place in shade.

Seedlings are delicate; grow them initially in dappled shade, avoiding the midday sun, and protect them from drying winds. Water and inspect daily.

Peat discs, micro pots or root trainers

Large seeds can be individually sown into micro pots or peat discs which give each seedling enough space to become well established. They can then be planted into their final flowering position.

Pre-soak peat discs and stand them on a tray for ease of watering. Place the seed into the pre-formed hole. When the roots appear through the netting the plant is ready to be transplanted. The manufacturers recommend that the plant should be transplanted complete with the net which makes transplanting a very simple operation and the plant suffers no root disturbance.

Peat discs

Alternatively, fill micro pots with the same soil mixture as for seed trays and sow the seeds. When the roots just start to appear the plant is well established and it is time to transplant it. Water well so you can remove the root ball intact with minimum root disturbance.

Use root trainers particularly for tree seeds as this allows the tap root to develop successfully. Root trainers can be unclipped to allow the tree seedling to be removed without disturbing the roots.

Watering

Germinating seedlings need to be watered using a mist sprayer or vey fine sprinkler which improves the success rate. Use any pump action spray container. Larger seedlings can be watered successfully with an old washing up bottle. The nozzle can be directed at the soil and delivers plenty of water without flattening the plants.

Transplanting

As transplanting is a shock to plants the aim is to minimize trauma and establish the plant quickly in its new site. Place in prepared soil and water in well. Transplant your own seedlings when they are large enough to handle at the 'four leaf' stage. The first two leaves produced are the 'cotyledons' or embryonic leaves, and are quickly followed by true leaves which have the characteristic look of the plant. When these are fully opened you can transplant seedlings either to the open ground or to individual pots. Before transplanting make sure the plants are well watered.

Most nursery seedlings are grown under shade net so once in your garden they must be gradually brought out into full light before planting or, better still, shade once planted. Gradually reduce the shading over a week.

After care

Water regularly and carefully as over-watering rots the plants and washes out the soil nutrient. Feed with an all purpose complete soluble fertilizer according to the manufacturer's instructions.

Remove the dead flowers before they have a chance to set seeds. Making seed drains the plants energy. Dead heading also stimulates the plant to produce more new blooms and prolong the flowering period. Some plants, such as Alyssum and Petunia, become long and straggly and will tolerate being cut back to 5-10 cm to flower a second time.

While the plants are still growing well and before the weather warms up take cuttings of Geranium, Busy Lizzie and herbs to keep as house plants over the summer.

Problem prevention

In conditions of warmth and high humidity seedlings can be infected by fungus which will rot and kill them. This is known as 'damping off'. Avoid this problem by using clean equipment, new compost and not overcrowding the seedlings.

Buying plants from nurseries

Inspect plants carefully; look out for mealy bug and vine weevil. *See Pests and Dangers Section*. Remove the root ball from the pot if possible and check for pests, slugs and root mealy bug. Reject plants with masses of roots emerging from the base of the container. Despite the temptation it is better to buy plants which have not started flowering. All the evidence suggests that these survive the shock of transplanting better and go on to produce bigger and better plants.

Taking cuttings

Introduction

This is a much easier and quicker process in the region than elsewhere in the world, since the warmth and humidity stimulates plant growth. The same growth can be achieved in weeks that might take months in Northern Europe. Many shrubs and climbers will flower from cuttings within six weeks. From seed, even annuals take 8-12 weeks to flower so cuttings are very worthwhile. In addition you know exactly what you are growing as your new plant is a clone of the original. Cuttings can be taken throughout the year, however, the best time is in the autumn and early spring when plants are vigorously growing.

The objective with all propagation methods is to reduce the trauma to the plant as much as possible whilst encouraging the plant to produce new roots. To achieve this you need to create a micro-climate of high humidity, avoiding hot drying winds and strong sunlight. Reduce contamination from fungus and moulds by using clean equipment and soil and clearing up dead plant material. Protect against insect attack.

Stem Cuttings

Plant material

Take cuttings from a good healthy plant with lots of vigorous new growth. An actively growing, non-flowering side shoot is ideal. The majority of shrubs root most quickly from a semi-hard wood stem.

This is a piece of stem half way between brown and green but still slightly flexible. Hard wood stems, all brown, are slower but more tolerant of casual treatment; experiment with both types of plant material. Initially cut through the hard wood area and immerse the stem in water immediately. To prepare the cuttings for planting trim off the base of the cut stem, at an angle, just below a leaf bud. Pinch out the terminal bud, together with any flowers and side shoots. Strip off most of the leaves leaving a pair or two near the tip. Removing the leaves reduces water loss, but the stem needs some leaves to manufacture food. Dip the cut end in to fresh hormone rooting powder, which greatly improves the success rate though it is not essential.

Soil

The soil should drain freely and yet be moisture retentive. Commercial nurseries use a mix of half peat moss and half vermiculite or perlite. Dry perlite or vermiculite floats to the surface and peat can be difficult to wet. It is much easier to mix and moisten the soil before filling the pots.

Planting

Choose a large plastic flower pot or similar container, approximately 20 cm diameter and fill two thirds full of soil. The large volume of soil acts as a reservoir and stops the pot drying out too quickly.

Make a generous hole in the soil and place the cutting in the hole so approximately two thirds of its length is in the soil. Place four to five cuttings in the pot, giving each enough room so that you can remove them later without damaging its neighbour.

Cover the pot loosely with a clear plastic bag, so the air can circulate and the leaves don't touch the sides. Use short sticks or stiff wire to make a frame to keep the plastic away from the plants.

Stand the pot in a saucer in a sheltered, shady place and leave it undisturbed for a week, filling the saucer to keep the soil

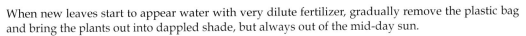

moist. At the end of the week remove the plastic bag, remove any dropped leaves or obviously dead cuttings. Re-cover and leave for 6-8 weeks.

When new leaves start to appear water with very dilute fertilizer, gradually remove the plastic bag and bring the plants out into dappled shade, but always out of the mid-day sun.

Potting on

When the cuttings start to produce new leaves or roots appear from the bottom of the pot the cuttings are ready to transplant. Water the pot well so the soil is 'plastic' and won't crack off the new roots as you tip out the pot. If all your cuttings have taken remove the biggest and best plants first at the expense of the weaker ones. Transplant into individual pots and grow on until the plant has a well established root ball. Finally plant into a well prepared final site and shade the plant for three to four days after transplanting with shade net or an umbrella. This is well worth doing since if you can prevent wilting it will continue to grow unchecked and become an established plant very rapidly.

Rooting in water

This method is suitable mainly for soft, fleshy plants, such as Busy Lizzie, Impatiens Portulaca, Basil and Mint. It also works well on shrubby plants, such as Vinca, *Catharanthus,* and on the blue-flowered climber Jacquemontia. Use a stem tip approximately 4-6 cm long, having stripped off the lower leaves and pinched out the terminal bud and any flowers. Half submerge the cuttings in a pot filled with normal tap water. Root formation is improved by excluding the light using dark brown glass or an opaque pot. Remove any dead stems and change the water regularly. When the stems produce roots pot into individual pots and cover with plastic for 7-10 days until the plant is established.

Taking cuttings is a very satisfying way of making a more unusual collection of plants with varieties not widely available at the garden nurseries. If you see a delectable plant in a private or public garden always ask if you may take a cutting. Refusal is rare and more likely you will be rewarded with a gift of an already established plant.

17

Most plants grown in the region are very resistant to pests and the small amount of damage can normally be tolerated. Some such as mealy bug attack specific plants in the spring and autumn and can be largely controlled by physical means. Gardens naturally attract wildlife and insects which greatly adds to their enjoyment and interest. Just a few pose a possible danger.

Preventing pests

Clear up dead plant material around all plants to reduce hiding places for weevils, woodlice and mites. Remove individual affected leaves at the first sign of attack. Check nursery plants very carefully for signs of infestation and isolate all new plants for a few days before planting them amongst existing plants. Keep equipment and pots clean by washing them in soapy water and drying them in direct sun light. Close bags of peat and compost. In addition, while not always practical, plants and seedlings can be covered with mosquito net. This is a very cheap and effective protection, widely available and environmentally friendly. Cut up a bed net to the appropriate size, prop it up with sticks and weigh it down with stones.

Insecticides

There are two types of insecticides, one works by coming into contact with the pests as they crawl over the treated surface. The other, systemic, is absorbed into the plant tissue and transported through the entire plant. Systemic insecticides are most useful for sap sucking insects.

Several chemicals are no longer available in Europe to the home gardener. While these may still be available in the region for agricultural purposes the home gardener should not use them. Check labels on the packets and bottles before purchasing.

Banned garden chemicals in insecticides in Europe

Chlorpyriphos, Dimethoate, Lindane, Malathion, Permethrin, Pirimicarb, Pirimiphos-methyl, Resmethrin, Rotenone.

Permitted garden chemicals in insecticides in Europe

Acetamiprid, Bifenthrin, Pyrethrin
Metaldehyde - permitted chemical slug pellets

Biological controls are now popular in Europe but are not yet available in the region.

CAUTION. Garden insecticides are poisonous. Treat them with care as you would any other toxic substance. Store them in safe places, make up small quantities and use them immediately. Wash your hands and equipment after use.

Pests and diseases

Aphids

Aphids, including greenfly and black fly, cluster on new buds and stems sucking the plant juices and exuding a sticky honey dew. The plant is weakened and leaves and buds are distorted. The honey dew is often colonized by sooty moulds. Regularly wash off the aphids with soapy water. Aphids seem to prefer a shady site, so drag pot plants into the sun and cut back over head trees. Organic gardeners in Australia have discovered that a spay made of boiled Lantana leaves is very effective as an aphid insecticide. Collect 0.5 kg of leaves and boil them up in 1.5 lt water. Strain off the liquid and dilute with an equal quantity of clean water and the insecticide is ready to use.

Birds

Gardens adjacent to open areas may be visited by groups of Grey Francolin, the small partridge like birds. Part of their diet is young shoots and seedlings which they can completely destroy ruining a seasons hard work. They also like to dig up newly sown beds and compost scattering soil and newly planted plants everywhere. Once they have found a good food source they come back repeatedly. Protect plants with netting propped up on sticks to keep it off the leaves. Once the plants are established the birds are less attracted.

Caterpillars

Pick off by hand and check the underside of leaves for further eggs and rub these away.

Lantana Fungus

Check for yellow spots on the leaves or dead patches which will appear a month after the plant is infected. The fungus will usually kill the plant and as there is no cure, remove the plant at the first signs before it infects other Lantanas in the area. The spores are spread by wind and rain but in a walled garden or isolated balcony it generally isn't a problem.

Leaf-Cutting Bees

Circular pieces of uniform size are removed from the leaf edges by leaf-cutting bees which use the leaves for nest building. Mosquito net the plant for several days until the bee moves off to another plant source. Alternatively swat the bees; usually only one or two individuals are active first thing in the morning.

Leaf Miners

Larvae of various flies which tunnel through the leaves leaving white irregular trails or white or brown blotched area on the leaves. Young plants are particularly vulnerable. Spray with one of the permitted chemicals. Once the leaves mature and are tougher it is less of a problem.

Locusts

Eat large areas of leaf leaving only the mid rib. Search out individuals and remove them.

Locust

Mealy Bugs

There are several different types of mealy bugs, however, all are white soft-bodied wingless insects often with white fine threads trailing from their bodies. White fluffy material appears in the leaf and stem joints especially on new growth. They particularly like Hibiscus but can be found on new growth of many plants. Their honey dew excretions are often colonized by sooty mold as with aphids.

A simple, effective remedy is to wash off the mealy bugs with a jet of water. This needs to be done weekly. Or wash the plant using a soft tooth brush in soapy water. Mix two teaspoons of washing up liquid in 4 lt of water, the soap helps to break down the waxy coat. This solution can also be used on root mealy bugs which tend only to be a problem in pot plants; immerse the whole pot in soapy water for 15 minutes then in fresh water.

Washing or spraying off mealy bug is usually sufficient and will keep them under control in the spring and autumn when they are most active. Spraying with the permitted chemicals is of limited use because their waxy coats protect them from contact sprays. Some plants are more resistant, such as the single flowered Hibiscus.

Scale Insects

Flat, usually gray-brown or green, oval discs attached to stems and lower leaf surfaces. The insects can be wiped off using damp cotton wool moistened with nail varnish remover.

Slugs

Dark shady permanently moist places such as under the shade net areas of nurseries often have slugs. Don't bring them home! Before you buy plants carefully inspect the pot base and the area where the plant was. Once home isolate new plants and take them out of the pot and inspect them for slugs. Treat with slug pellets containing metaldehyde.

Vine Weevil

A grey-black beetle that feeds at night making irregular holes in the leaf margins. The maggot-like larvae eat the roots and stems of shrubs and annuals below ground causing the plant to grow slowly, wilt and even die. Damage occurs over a long period and it is difficult to control. Adults are active at dawn and dusk. When disturbed they usually drop off the plant and play dead and can easily be killed. Established plants can withstand the damage but if the infestation is bad spray at dusk with a bug spray containing pyrethrin.

White Flies

Small white flying insects suck plant juices and exude sticky honey dew. The immature scale-like nymphs are immobile and can be wiped off localized infestations.

Woodlice

Also known as slaters or pill bugs and are grey or brown-grey and feed mainly on dead material. They also attack seedlings, however, eating holes in the leaves and shoot tips. Generally they are harmless and can be controlled by clearing up plant debris. Seedlings can be protected by sprinkling methiocarb slug pellets round the area.

Dangers in the garden

The dangers from the few animals which pose a threat can largely be overcome by taking sensible precautions, i.e. wear closed shoes and use gloves for gardening. You should also keep the garden tidy, store pots upside down and check carefully before moving equipment and materials which have lain undisturbed for any length of time. As well as animal dangers there are several poisonous plants. Avoid using these, particularly those with attractive berries, in gardens where there are children. Always wear gloves and wash your hands after handling plants.

Redback Spider or Black Widow

Widespread in the region particularly found along the coast. There are two local species and one probably introduced from Australia. These are small black spiders with dark red markings on the back like two triangles pointing towards each other giving the shape of an hour glass. The spider likes to hide in shady places and builds its web in places where half the web is in sunlight and the other part is in shade. They can be found in any undisturbed places, plastic flower pots, garden tools and outdoor furniture. The bite is not usually noticed until it starts to swell when two tiny puncture marks become visible.

Bill Wilks

It is very painful with aches, fever, nausea, raised blood pressure and even difficulty in breathing. Seek medical attention. Bites while painful are not nomally serious and victims normally recover in two days.

Scorpions

Black scorpions look more fearsome but the transparent ones have a more powerful venom. They are commonly found in gardens. They are usually active at night, especially in the summer, sleeping by day behind sacks of compost and empty pots. The sting is intensely painful and generally localized. Some victims may suffer further ill affects including diminished co-ordination and even hemorrhages and convulsions. Seek medical attention.

Bill Wilks

Snakes

Are rare in gardens and do their best to avoid contact with humans. There are, however, several poisonous snakes in the region all belonging to the viper family. The Sawscale or Carpet Viper hisses a loud warning so is easily avoided. The Sand Viper hunts its prey by lying just underneath the sand so could possibly be trodden on by accident. Viper bites cause localized swelling. Seek medical attention. The most common snake is the slender Wadi Racer which, as its name suggests, is a fast mover usually seen shooting off in the opposite direction. In wadis it eats toads but in garden its diet is mainly insects and geckos and is harmless.

ANNUALS

Tall blue Salvia, Snapdragons and Petunia

Growing annuals is a delight and the long winter season in Oman and the UAE is always an inspiration for gardeners. The range of plants is extensive with new ones being introduced each year. Whether you grow them from seed or buy plants from the nurseries, you can have a wonderfully colourful garden all through the winter months and selected plants will extend the season through the summer months.

When to sow seeds

In Europe the seed packets warn to wait until all danger of frost has past. In Oman and the UAE packets should say, "**Warning;** wait until night temperatures are consistently below 30°C". This is particularly critical for seedlings, as night time temperatures higher than 30°C cause plants to use up more energy in transpiration than they can make during the day on their small immature leaves.

You can get a head start by sowing seeds indoors in the cool of the air-conditioning. Choose heat resistant plants so you can plant them out even when the temperatures are still high. If you leave them indoors the relatively high temperatures of indoor A/C plus low light levels (tinted glass, shaded windows) will make the seedlings tall, spindly and useless.

By mid to end of October night temperatures should drop and you can then plant the bulk of seeds, but check on a min/max thermometer. There is a lot of local variation and the winter seems to be starting later.

Strong light levels of the region ensure plants flower quickly, even very small plants, and produce a fantastic display all through the winter months.

What not to grow

'The lots of lovely green leaves but no flowers syndrome'

With winter temperatures in the region similar to a good European summer it's assumed that plants which do well there will be equally successful here. A large group of plants, however, need regular night temperatures of below 15°C to flower well. As the minimum night time temperature in much of the region rarely drops below 18°C plants produce abundant leaves but few, if any, flowers. Some of the most popular plants such as Sweet Peas, Nasturtiums and Californian Poppies need cool night time temperatures. The local climatic conditions will depend whether you should grow the following:

Arctotis hybrida - Arctotis
Dimorphotheca species - African Daisy
Eschscholzia californica - Californian Poppies
Gerbera - Transvaal Daisy
Lathyrus odoratus - Sweet Pea
Penstemon gloxinioides - Penstemon
Tropaeolum majus - Nasturtium

Other plants require long daylight length to flower, such as Lobelia; this produces trailing stems of leaves but doesn't flower well until about March, when it becomes a race between flowering and being killed by the increasing heat. Alternatively plant early in the autumn so they flower before the days shorten, once stimulated to flower they will usually continue to do so. The relationship between daylight length and temperature is very complicated. *Petunia*, which also requires long daylight length to flower, will flower in short days as long as the temperature is over 20°C.

What to grow

The range of annuals grown during the winter months increases each year and the nurseries have a good stock but tend to stick to the tried and tested. There are many plants that could do well; for the price of a packet of seeds it's worth a try. The following list is made up of plants seen successfully growing in the region. Where possible the variety is also specified, as characteristics vary and not all varieties do well.

Ageratum houstonianum - **Floss Flower**

Garden varieties are mostly compact, low growing at 15-30 cm high with a spread of 23-30 cm. The flowers are deep blue, pale blue or white depending on the variety. The 'powder puff' flowers are borne in clusters giving the plant a fluffy appearance and flower continuously over a long period.

  The tiny seeds require light to germinate so just press the seeds into the surface of the compost to anchor them. Germination 7-10 days at 21-29°C. Plant 15-20 cm apart in well prepared rich soil in full sun or light shade. Under conditions of high humidity powdery mildew can be a problem. Avoid wetting the leaves or planting densely but keep them well watered.

Alyssum maritimum. Syn. *Lobularia maritima* - **Sweet Alyssum**

Low growing, small plant height 3-6 cm, spread 8-12 cm. Densely branched with linear grey-green leaves. The flower colours are white, blue-purple or pink. The four-petaled flowers are borne in profusion which produces a show of solid colour.

  Scatter seeds on the surface as they require light to germinate. Germination 7-30 days, the majority will germinate in 15 days, at 15-29°C. Transplant to their flowering positions when they are large enough to handle. Plant in full sun at the edge of the border or in containers. As the plants become leggy cut halfway back for a second crop of flowers. Alternatively, regularly dead head by trimming back lightly with scissors. Easy to grow, dependable plant which re-seeds itself.

Amaranthus tricolor - Amaranthus, Joseph's Coat

Large bushy plants 60-90 cm. Grown for their lovely coloured leaves of red, yellow, orange, dark brown and lime-green. A well know variety is 'Joseph's coat'.

Just cover the seeds with soil as light aids germination. Germination takes 8-10 days at 21-30°C. Plant 60 cm apart in full sun. Does well even in poor soils. It is drought tolerant and is an excellent container plant.

Antirrhinum - Snapdragon

A bushy plant with a wide range of flower colours; white, lemon through orange, pinks to mauve and deep red. There is also a wide range of size from 15–90 cm, however the 30 cm compact bedding plants such as *Antirrhinum nanum* 'Dwarf Bedding' seem to do well in the region and germinate in high temperatures 21-30°C.

Surface sow the seeds as they require light to germinate. Pinch out the tips early to produce lots of side shoots with several blooms. Keep dead heading to prolong flowering. Does well in sandy soils.

Calendula officinalis - Pot Marigold

An easy to grow annual. A bushy plant which grows to 30-60 cm high with the same spread. The flowers are shades of yellow or orange, often double, 8-10 cm across. Leaves are fleshy with a pleasant spicy fragrance and both the leaves and flowers can be used in salads. The petals can also be used as a substitute for saffron to colour rice.

Plant the large seeds directly where they are to flower and cover with 6 mm of soil. Germination 10-14 days, temperature 18 -29 °C. Thin plants out to 30-40 cm apart and plant in full sun. They are tolerant of poor soil as long as it is well drained.

Catharanthus roseus - Vinca, Madagascar Periwinkle

Small erect annual or short lived perennial bush reaching 75 cm. Grown for its continuous display of flowers even in the height of summer. The flowers are dark pink, pink, white or white with a red eye. Pink flowered forms seem to be the toughest. Self sown plants revert to pink.

Just cover the seeds, germination 14-21 days, temperature 23-29°C. Thrives in full sun, is medium salt tolerant and very drought tolerant. Plants tend to become straggly, try pruning back to the lowest leaf. Alternatively sow annually as the flush of flowers in the first year is the best. Can also be propagated very easily from cuttings and flowers quickly on small plants.

Celosia - Cockscomb

There are two species of *Celosia*. *C. cristata* is the crested type and the flowers resemble a piece of coral. *C. plumosa* has loose and feathery plum-shaped flowers. Both have a range of flower colours; yellow, orange, red and deep magenta red. The leaves are green or bronze. Height 15-60 cm, depending on the variety.

Sow seeds directly in the flowering site or in individual pots as they flower less well if they suffer root disturbance as seedlings. Just cover the seeds, which germinate in 8-14 days at 21-30°C. They prefer a rich soil in full sun. The flowers are long lasting but remove them once they are past their best and new flowers will be produced well into the early summer.

Chrysanthemum annual species – Annual Chrysanthemum, Painted Daisy

Chrysanthemum carinatum is a bushy plant with daisy-like flowers of red, white and yellow. Many of the flowers are made up of multicolored rings with orange-brown centres. *Chrysanthemum paludosum* is 15 cm in height with white flowers and yellow centres, and is often used for edging.

Just cover the seeds with 3 mm of soil. Germination 7-30 days at 18 -29°C depending on the variety. Thrives in full sun and does well in poor sandy soils.

Coleus blumei - Coleus

Grown for its wonderful exotic multi-coloured leaves of red, green, yellow, white, pink and orange depending on the variety.

Surface sow the small seed and water by misting so the seed is not disturbed, then loosely

cover with a plastic bag so the seeds never dry out. Germination 10-20 days at 21-30°C. Lower temperatures or drying out inhibit germination. Plant in rich soil in partial shade about 30 cm apart. Pinch out the growing tip and remove the flower spikes to produce bushy plants. Before the summer heat take cuttings, which will root in water, to use as indoor plants over the summer.

Coreopsis tinctoria - Golden Tickseed

A slender plant with feathery foliage 30-50 cm tall depending on the variety. The masses of daisy-like flowers are traditionally yellow, orange and red; new varieties include white, pink and dark burgundy. A very easy to grow annual, the yellow forms are the easiest.

Sow seeds in flowering position and just cover with compost. Germination 21-30 days at 20-25°C; some new varieties require cooler germination temperatures, check the planting instructions. Plant in full sun. The plants are tolerant of poor soils and once established are drought resistant. Plant in a big group for maximum effect.

Cosmos bipinnatus - **Cosmos**

Tall plants, 45-90 cm with feathery foliage producing abundant daisy-like flowers of white, shades of pink to dark red.

Germination 7-14 days at 18-29 °C. Space about 15 cm apart. Dead head to prolong flowering. Both heat and drought tolerant and do well in sandy soils.

Dianthus - **Pinks**

Bushy compact plants growing 30 cm tall with a similar spread. Flower profusely in the cooler months in colours of red, pink or white and bi-colours.

Just cover the seeds with compost, germination 14-30 days at 18-29°C. Space the plants 20-30 cm apart. Tolerates poor sandy soils and prefers dry conditions. High humidity and over-watering can lead to the plants rotting off. Plants that survive the summer will flower again in the autumn.

Gaillardia - **Blanket Flowers**

Large plants reaching 20-45 cm, with a similar spread depending on the variety. Abundant daisy-shaped flowers in shades of red, orange or yellow with a contrasting centre. They have a very long flowering period, even over the summer.

Press the seeds lightly into the soil surface as they need light to germinate. Germination 4-10 days at 21-30°C. Space plants 30 cm apart in full sun. The plants are drought tolerant and grow well in poor soils. Remove dead flower heads to encourage new blooms. With some shading they will survive the summer to bloom well again the following autumn.

Gazania - **Gazania**

Low growing spreading plants 10-25 cm, depending on the variety, with narrow green or silver leaves. The abundant dazzling flowers are daisy-like and come in a range of colours; white, cream, yellow and shades of orange, with a contrasting dark centre. The petals close at night or in cloudy weather.

Just cover seeds with 3 mm of soil. Germination takes 4-12 days at 18-25°C. Best germinate indoors in A/C conditions or wait until mid-winter for successful sowing. Plant in full sun and dead head for repeat flowering. Likes well drained sandy soil, heat and drought tolerant and can often survive the summer and flower again in the autumn.

Gomphrena globosa - Globe Amaranth

Bushy, spreading plants usually 30-40 cm tall. The clover-like flowers have a papery texture and can be white, pale pink or dark red-purple.

Sow the seeds where they are to flower and press into the surface as they need light to germinate. Germination approximately two weeks at 21-30°C. Plants tolerate poor soils, heat and drought. They die out in mid summer but often self-sown seedlings appear in the autumn.

Impatiens walleriana - Busy Lizzie

A bushy plant with soft succulent stems producing a profusion of flowers of white, salmon, rose, pink or red.

Light aids germination. Press the tiny seed into the compost and water by misting as the seeds and seedlings are delicate. Germination 10-21 days at 21-29°C. Plant out in a shaded site, in rich soil with plenty of organic material, such as peat moss. When the temperature rises take cuttings which will root in water and keep them over summer as house plants.

Ipomoea annual climbing species

Climbing *Ipomoea* are very fast growing, reaching three metres. The twining stems support large heart shaped leaves and masses of trumpet shaped flowers. There are many different varieties available with red, white, pink, blue or purple flowers.

Ipomoea alba - Moon Flower

The white flowers start to open at dusk and are fully open by the early evening, emitting a wonderful scent, great in pots on a patio. Sow the seed in early autumn as the plants are slower to flower than other varieties.

Ipomoea tricolor - Morning Glory,

is the best known *Ipomoea* and a well known cultivar is 'Heavenly Blue' with large sky blue flowers. Originally the flowers faded by midday, hence the common name; new hybrid varieties have flowers that last all day.

Ipomoea quamoclit - Cyprus Vine

syn. *I. pennata* has very different leaves to other *Ipomoea*, they are made of many slim leaflets, giving the leaves a feathery appearance. The flowers of hybrid varieties are white, pink or brilliant scarlet red. Self-sown seedlings always revert to red. A very heat-tolerant variety, can be planted in late winter to flower into the summer and following autumn.

Pre-soak the seeds overnight and cover with 6 mm of soil in individual pots or in situ. Germinates 5-10 days at 21-30°C. Plant *I. alba* and *I. tricolor* in the autumn. *I. tricolor* will benefit from morning shade, to prolong the flowers. All do well in poor sandy soil; too much fertilizer or rich soil makes the plants produce masses of leaves and few flowers. Excellent in containers with a wigwam support system. Regularly pinch out the terminal bud to encourage branched growth. The seeds are worth collecting of all varieties as flowering qualities do not seem to diminish greatly with second generation seeds.

Nicotiana tobacum - Tobacco

Has escaped into the wild in Dhofar and is also a cultivated crop in the region. It grows over a metre tall and has small pink flowers. Grow it at the back of a border for the lush green leaves. Plants self-seed.

Nicotiana - Flowering Tobacco

New dwarf garden cultivars are short, 30-45 cm, with a compact habit. The flowers remain open all day and have a wide range of colours; white, pink, peach, red, purple and even lime green. Excellent around patios for their night time fragrance.

Light aids germination so press the seeds into the compost and mist spray to keep the seeds moist and in place. Germination takes 5-12 days at 21-30°C. Plant out in full sun in good soil.

Pelargonium - Geraniums

Probably one of the most popular European summer plants so consequently there are hundreds of varieties. Flower colours include white, pink, salmon, red and bi-coloured flowers. Trailing varieties are now available from seed. They do well in the region during the winter months, especially after December when the increasing daylight length encourages them to flower. Tolerant of full sun and high heat but are very susceptible to humid conditions, so don't survive over the summer outdoors.

Geraniums are slow to bloom from seed, taking about 16 weeks from germination, so they need to be started indoors in July or August to get maximum winter flowering. Use a well draining compost (add vermiculite or course sand) and just cover the seeds. Keep in a light place and at a constant temperature as both conditions aid germination. Germination 7-21 days at 21-30°C. Once germinated ensure the compost is moist at all times but not wet as plants are very susceptible to rot in the early stages. Plant out in sandy, well drained soil. Dead head and feed regularly for a continuous display of flowers. Ideal for pots and containers. Take cuttings which will root in water to keep over summer as attractive flowering house plants.

Petunia - Petunia

Petunias are well adapted to the hot conditions of the region and flower non-stop from October to end of May, or even June. Two main types are available; the large flowered Grandiflora, 10-12 cm blooms, and the smaller Multiflora with an abundance of smaller, 8 cm blooms. In addition there are trailing types of both varieties. The colour range is extensive; white through pinks, mauves, reds and bi-colours. The flowers can be single, double and frilled.

Petunia seed is tiny. Sow the seed very thinly so that the plants have enough space to develop and can be planted directly into the flowering site without an intermediate stage. The seeds need light to germinate and must not be disturbed, so press into the soil surface and keep it moist by misting. Germination 7-10 days at 21- 30°C. Pinch out the tips early to encourage bushy plants. Space 15 cm apart in full sun in well drained sandy soil. Dead head and feed regularly to maintain a constant display. If the plants become straggly trim them back by half for a second display. Try a second sowing in November or December for a good display into the early summer. Don't collect the seed as the second generation seed produces very poor plants.

Portulaca - Sun Plant

A low growing 15 cm tall with a spread up to 60 cm. The cone-shaped flower can be single or double and the colour range is extensive; magenta, several shades of pink, white, peach, yellow and orange flowers. The flowers open in the sun and close in the shade or at dusk.

Portulaca can be grown from cuttings, placed in water, or seed. More exotic larger flowered and double types are generally grown from seed as they tend to die out in the winter. Surface sow seeds as they need light to germinate. Germination 10-21 days at 21-30°C. Does well in full sun, poor sandy soils and in hot dry conditions with minimal water. A really valuable plant in the summer months.

Salvia species

Salvia splendens varieties have flowers in a range of colours from scarlet through burgundy, purple and shades of pink. Bushy plants with dark green foliage approximately 30 cm tall.

Just cover the seeds, which germinate in 21-24 days at 21-30°C. Keep seedlings just moist to avoid problems of dampening off (rotting). Plant out in sun or partial shade in fertile well-drained soil. Reliable and long-flowering, trim off the spent flowers in January for a second burst of flowers in February/March.

Salvia patens, 'Cambridge Blue', though a perennial, flowers in the first year so can be grown as an annual. It has wonderful blue flowers on slender stems. Ideal temperatures for germination are between 15-20°C. Start indoors in cool A/C, takes 14-30 days to germinate. Gradually acclimatize to warmer temperatures. Flowers in the winter only. Not easy but worth the effort for the results.

Tagetes - Marigolds

Erect bushy plants ranging from 20-75 cm depending on the type. Flowers can be daisy-shaped or pompom types in white, yellow and shades of orange. Although all do well in hot dry conditions the smaller flowered varieties are easiest to grow.

Plant directly into the flowering site and just cover with soil. Germination 7-10 days at 21-30ºC. Plant out in full sun, does well in poor sandy soils. Excessive feeding and moisture encourages leafy growth and less flowers. Dead head to prolong blooming or repeat sowings for long display.

Zinnia

Mainly tall plants with a height of 30-60 cm. There are a range of flower shapes; single daisy-type, doubles and pompoms depending on the variety. The colour range is extensive; white, yellow, orange, pink and red.

If possible plant in situ or sow seeds in individual pots as they are very intolerant of root disturbance. Germination is rapid, 3-7 days at 21-30ºC. Plant out in full sun in well drained soil. Avoid wetting the leaves as they are susceptible to rot. Pinch out the growing tip to promote side branches, dead head and feed to maintain flowering. Zinnias are very heat-tolerant and are often planted late so that they are in full bloom into May and June when most other plants have finished. The new dwarf types such as 'Profusion mixed' (see picture below) are shorter and make compact bushy plants with a longer flowering period and will flower all summer.

HERBS

Tall Basils and ground cover Mint

Herbs can be grown throughout the winter months but most will die out in summer. Treat as annuals or take cuttings in spring before the weather warms up and grow them indoors, in a well lit, air conditioned environment over the summer. Many herbs come from the Mediterranean and prefer dry soil conditions. Plant in sandy, free-draining soils in open ground or unglazed clay pots. Peat based potting composts are too moisture retentive and may cause the roots to rot. Increase drainage by adding sweet sand, vermiculite or perlite. *See Soil Section.*

Allium schoenoprasum - Chives

Grow from imported seed or divide established pots bought from the supermarket. Does well in mid-winter in dappled or partly shady conditions as it requires cool temperatures to flourish and becomes spindly as temperatures increase.

Coriandrum - Coriander, Chinese Parsley

A plant with dark cut leaves, reaching 75 cm with white or pink flowers. Widely grown in the region and easily mistaken for flat leaved parsley. Coriander can be grown either for the leaves or seed.

For leaf production plant in a partially shady place as this reduces the chance of the plant bolting (flowering prematurely), which will stop the plant developing new leaves. For seed, plant in full sun.

Plant the seed in situ as it dislikes root disturbance, having a very long tap root, and just cover with soil. Keep moist, germination takes around 14 days. Once the plant has reached 10-15 cm the leaves can be plucked. Remove any flower heads as they develop.

Many new cultivars are bolt resistant - 'Leisure', 'Santo' and others are 'cut and come again' - 'Calypso' - where the plant can be trimmed to the ground and will re-sprout usually up to three times. Sow a small amount every three weeks for good leaf supply.

Mentha - Common Mint

Grow from locally bought bunches of mint which often have roots attached. Stems will root in water. Plant the rooted cuttings in a pot and cover with plastic and place in a cool shady place until the plant is established. Does best in a shady site. During the summer the leaves die back but it often reappears from live roots as the temperatures reduce.

Ocimum species – Basil

There are over 30 species of basil, some with green leaves, some with purple and a wide variation in flavours and colour, look out for interesting types to raise from seed.

Ocimum basilicum - Sweet Green Basil

The most commonly grown annual type which is traditionally used to make pesto. A fast easy to grow bushy shrub, with soft green leaves and a mild flavour.

Plant the seeds in early autumn, just covering them with a sprinkle of soil. Germination 7-14 days at 21-30°C. Pinch out the growing tip to encourage side shoots and remove flowers. Does really well outdoors in the winter months in dappled shade and often survives the summer. Must be kept well-watered and fed regularly to produce really vigorous growth. Bring some plants indoors in the summer as insurance. It can also be started from cuttings which root easily in water.

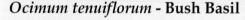

Ocimum tenuiflorum - Bush Basil

A large, easy to grow vigorous plant reaching 90 cm. It has stiff stems becoming woody with age and smaller dark green leaves with white flowers and dark red purple bracts. The leaves have a very strong flavour.

Widely grown in the region, grow from locally collected seed or cuttings which root in water easily. Tolerant of full sun and poor soils and grows as a perennial surviving the summer. It is often used as a ground cover plant under trees or trimmed into a relaxed hedge.

Origanum species - Oregano, Marjoram

There are over 20 species and many different varieties with round and pointed leaves which can be green, yellow or variegated. Flavour can also vary; *Origanum vulgre* or Greek Oregano has a strong pungent taste where as *Origanum marjorana,* commonly known as Sweet or Knotted Marjoram, has a much milder flavour.

Easy to grow from surface sown seed. Germination 3-14 days at 20-30°C or re-pot supermarket pots into a larger container of well-drained soil. Grows well in full sun in the winter months, regularly feed with liquid fertilizer and pinch out tips for a bushy plant. Leaves and flowers can be used in cooking.

Petroselinum crispum - Parsley

Grow either flat or the curly leafed type from seed annually. Use fresh seed and soak it for 12 hours prior to planting, to help germination which can be erratic, taking up to 28 days. Once the plants are growing well start harvesting. Feed regularly with liquid fertilizer for abundant leafy growth. The flat leafed variety has a longer growing season.

Salvia officinalis - Sage

Grey-leaved bushy plant which can reach 60-80 cm. Start annually from seed, *see Salvia splendens, Annuals.* Start early, indoors, in the autumn as plants take approximately three months before they are big enough to pick the leaves. Alternatively re-pot plants from the supermarket to grow on. Pinch out the growing tip to encourage basal growth and new foliage which is best for cooking.

GROUND COVER & GRASSES

There are a variety of ground cover plants, many are naturally low growing, with horizontally spreading branches. Others tolerate repeated clipping to keep them neat and bushy, making a dense cover.

Many ground cover plants make excellent container plants. Their robust nature allows them to flourish in the difficult conditions of a pot. Low spreading ones trail over the sides, upright plants form a dense green mass.

Alternanthera versicolor - Joseph's Coat, Parrot Leaf

Low growing spreading ground cover plant reaching approximately 20 cms but best clipped to keep it compact and bushy. There are several different forms; dark red, green and white, green and red. They all have insignificant white flowers.

Easy and trouble-free, hence its popularity in municipal plantings. Salt tolerance low, and requires good irrigation to keep it growing well or it becomes sparse and patchy. Thrives in sun or partial shade and looks good all year. Propagate by division or cuttings.

Asystasia gangetica - Corommandel

A trailing rambling plant with long stems which will act as ground cover, or will scramble over walls and fences. The leaves are a fresh green with a slightly downy feel to them. The bell shaped flowers can be white, cream or a lovely lilac colour flushed with darker purple and have a yellow throat. Flowers profusely through the winter months.

Establish in the autumn with the roots in shade if possible. Once established it is fast growing and rampant and can withstand the summer heat though it does burn and ceases to flower. The stems will root where they touch. Look for a rooted stem from an established plant or take cuttings, which will root in water.

'Ice Plant' types

Low growing succulents with daisy-like flowers which open in the sun and close at dusk. Though similar in appearance there are several species which make up this group.

Name	Spread	Height	Comment, flower colour
Carpobrotus edulis - **Hotentot Fig**	1m	25cm	triangular stems, sour but edible fruit, pink, pale yellow
Delosperma 'Alba'	60cm	12cm	snow white
Drosanthemum hispidum	45cm	12cm	lavender, rose
Lampranthus aurantiacus	45cm	15cm	orange (figured)
Lampranthus spectabilis	45cm	15cm	dark red-purple
Malephora crocea	45cm	15cm	red and orange

All thrive in full sun. Drought and salt tolerant, particularly *Carpobratus edulis* which is used in coastal plantings. During humid summer months the plants are vulnerable to rot and need minimal amounts of watering. Plant on free draining sandy soils to avoid any chance of waterlogged conditions. Despite summer die-back they usually revive in the winter. Propagate from cuttings.

Ipomoea species

Ipomoea batatas - Sweet Potato Vine

Dark green, heart-shaped leaves form a dense mat with long trailing stems radiating out. The garden hybrid has large vivid, variegated leaves of lime green and yellow. The pale pink flowers are sparse and insignificant.

Grows well in full sun, moderately drought and salt tolerant. With the hybrid variety prune out any runners which revert to the smaller dark green leaf of the original plant. Propagate from cuttings, establish before the summer.

Ipomoea pes-caprae - Camel or Goat's Foot Creeper

Thick trailing prostrate stems up to 12 m long. Shiny two-lobed leaves, with short-lived purple cone-shaped flowers.

Rampant and tough with high salt and drought tolerance. Can be planted on beach sands where it will spread to the high water mark. Excellent to grow where nothing else will, but can be a pest in a small garden. Propagate by cutting as seed doesn't set in the region.

Lantana montevidensis - Trailing Lantana

Low growing with long trailing stems. The leaves are small and saw toothed with the characteristic aromatic smell of Lantana. There are several types with different coloured flowers; white, yellow and purple. The flower clusters are spread all along the length of the stem. The main flowering period is during the winter months but it has sporadic flowers all year.

Does well on sandy soils and is moderately drought tolerant but has a low salt tolerance. Best planted in dappled shade as it burns in summer but recovers well in the winter. Requires careful watering during periods of high humidity as the stems are subject to rot. Can be subject to Lantana Fungus, *see Pests and Diseases*. Propagate by layering, trailing stems sometimes root where they touch. Alternatively use woody twigs as cuttings.

Ruellia tweediana - Wild Petunia

Vigorous upright plant reaching 90 cm with dark green leaves and pink, lilac or dark lilac flowers. The flowers are at their best in the morning, fading by late afternoon. Flowers best in the winter but has some flowers all year, except at the height of summer.

Does well in full sun and partial shade though it produces less flowers. Drought tolerant. Tends to become tall and straggly, trim to keep neat. The stems spread and root where they touch so it can be invasive and needs to be dug out. Propagate by dividing clumps

Sesuvium portulacastrum. Syn. *Portulaca portulacastrum*
Shoreline Sea-purslane

Green fleshy stems form a dense ground cover with an inconspicuous small pink flower. Very reliable, tolerates full sun and partial shade, very salt tolerant and can be next to the sea, and fast growing.

Each plant can spread up to a metre square, plant more closely for quicker cover. Often used by landscapers to stabilise banks of loose soil. Propagate by planting stems in the ground where they are to grow.

Tradescantia pallida. Syn. Setcreasea purpura
Purple Heart, Purple Queen

Dark red to purple stems 30 cm long lie horizontally along the ground creating complete cover. It has small pink three-petaled flowers on the stem tips especially over the winter months.

Very reliable and easy. Tolerates dappled shade but looks best in full sun. Easy to propagate from cuttings in water or directly into the soil.

Tradescantia spathacea. *Syn. Rhoeo discolo* - **Moses in a Cradle**

The fleshy pointed leaves are green on the upper side and deep purple-red on the underneath and form dense ground cover of about 30 cm in height. The small white flowers are cupped in dark purple bracts and flower all year.

Tolerates full sun but also does well in partial shade. Requires little maintenance and grows well in poor soils even in competition with tree roots. Grow easily from cuttings in sandy soils.

Wedelia trilobata - **Creeping Daisy**

Vigorous bright green stems spread over a wide area of up to 2 m, spangled with yellow daisy-like flowers borne singly on short stems. The leaves form a dense mat which at a distance looks like lawn.

Grows in full sun or partial shade but during high humidity in the summer the stems can rot and go black, best on well drained soils. Low salt tolerance and needs regular irrigation. Propagates easily by cuttings or layering. Also check mature plants for rooted nodes.

Grasses

Pennisetum setaceum – Fountain Grass

An elegant ornamental grass with slender arching leaves forming a dense clump 90 cm to 1.2 m high with a 60 cm spread. Two cultivars are widely grown in the region, 'African Fountain Grass' which is green with white seed heads and 'Rubrum' which has dark red leaves and pink-purple seed heads.

Easy and reliable and very tough, once it is established, also very drought tolerant. To keep the plant compact trim back to about 15 cm every six months, it will take 4-6 weeks to regenerate. Propagate by dividing large clumps into sections, it will also self-seed.

SHRUBS

In Oman and the UAE shrubs provide much of the colour and interest in gardens, many flower virtually continuously. With a wide variety to choose from it's quite possible to always have something in flower.

What to choose

As a first step look in the neighbouring gardens to see what does well. The local parks are also a good source of ideas. Recently planted parks give you a good indication of how quickly plants grow to maturity in the region. They also often contain innovative ideas and new varieties of plants.

When and how

Shrubs are best planted in the cooler months so they become well established before the summer heat. When planting large shrubs, such as Hibiscus, a 50 cm square area should ideally be prepared. Enrich the soil with organic material such as peat or compost to condition the soil and help retain moisture. Add organic manure or chemical fertilizers for nutriments, *see Soil Conditioners & Fertilizers for details*. Compost decomposes and should be replaced annually by lightly digging it into the surface. Fertilizers should be added monthly during the growing season of October to March. Regular watering is essential; a drip feed system is ideal and can be extended to water large containers as well as for direct soil planting.

Transplanting shrubs

Large shrubs and even small trees can be transplanted from one site to another successfully with a little time and effort, so even if you have to move you can take your garden with you.

Prune the plant to be moved, reducing the leaf area it has to support and making it easier to work round the plant. Dig a trench round the plant, encompassing as much of the root ball as it is feasible to lift. The lateral roots will be cut but vertical roots will be undamaged and will support the plant during this period. Backfill the trench round the plant with good quality soil and water well. This encourages the plant to make new lateral roots. Wait until there is some new leaf growth, approximately 7-10 days, then sever the roots beneath as deep as possible and slide the root ball onto a strong plastic sheet. It can now be lifted more easily and transplanted to the new site.

Place the root ball in a prepared hole making sure that the plant is vertical and that the new soil level is the same as the original. Trim off any torn or damaged roots and firm in the new soil. Water well and shade the plant for a couple of weeks to help it get established. Bury an inverted water bottle with the base cut off, or a length of pipe and water through it so the water gets well down into the soil to encourage vertical roots to anchor the plant in the new site.

Most shrubs and ground cover plants are readily propagated from cuttings in the autumn and spring. In some cases it's also possible to grow plants from seed where the plant produces abundant supplies of seed and can grow rapidly into a worthwhile plant.

The selection of plants listed below contains some of the most popular and robust plants available, as well as some more unusual ones. While the latter often have the drawback of looking poor in the summer months they come into their own during the winter with splendid displays of flowers. Their shape and form make for a more interesting garden which can otherwise look like any other green space.

Adenium species - Desert Rose

There are now about seven recognised species of *Adenium* and many further sub species and hybrids. ***Adenium obesum*** is the only one native to the region and it comes from Dhofar, Southern Oman. The flowers are shades of pink and the leaves are rounded. *A. obesum* in particular often has a very swollen base and wonderfully contorted branches. Rarely found in nurseries.

Commonly available are cultivated *Adenium* which have a range of flower colours from white all through the pink, red spectrum. All have tubular flowers made up of five petals borne on the branch tips. Height, depending on the type, 50 cm–2 m, spread similar dimensions. The shrubby varieties can be grown as a hedge.

Plant in full sun on free draining sandy soils with minimum watering, especially around the stem as it can be vulnerable to rotting. Only fertilize if the leaves are looking poor and yellow. One dose of half strength liquid fertilizer should be enough. Fertilizing causes the plant to produce soft sappy growth at the expense of flowers and makes it vulnerable to rot.

Propagate by cuttings to get an identical plant. By seed, the flower colour and plant shape will not be the same as the parent. Always use fresh seed. Just cover the seed with soil and loosely wrap the pot in a plastic bag to ensure the seed is always moist. Germination 5-10 days at 25-30°C. Once the plants germinate remove the covering and let the growing medium dry out a little. Plants from seed flower in 6-9 months. **The sap and all parts of the plant are very poisonous.**

Ali Al Abdullatif

Adenium obesum

Bougainvillea

If you had space for only one plant, Bougainvillea would be the first choice. It is wonderfully versatile and can be grown as a container plant, ground cover, hedging, a shrub or trained as a standard shrub or as a climbing plant.

The colour is provided by modified leaves at the base of the flower stalk called 'bracts'. In single forms three large and long-lasting bracts surround three thin tube-shaped flowers. Although insignificant the flowers give an 'eye' to the blooms of darker colours. Double forms have no flower, the multiple bracts all cluster together, giving intense bunches of colour. A disadvantage of the double form is the bracts do not naturally shed on fading and have to be removed by hand.

The diversity of colour is extensive, from pure white through a range of pale pink, yellow, orange, apricot to red, rich dark red and red-purple. As the bracts mature they often change shade or even colour which adds a further dimension to the colour range.

Generally Bougainvillea plants are not named in regional nurseries, but it is helpful to be aware that there are plants with distinctive growth habits.

Mainly tough and trouble free. Resistant to drought, but low salt tolerance. Bougainvillea thrive and flower best in full sun and in light well drained soil.

Ground cover

Several low-growing spreading varieties exist. Amongst these are two easily recognizable variegated types. 'Mary Palmer' has green and cream leaves, the new growth is tinged with pink and light pink bracts and 'Rainbow' has green and yellow leaves with pink and white bracts. Their stems tend to grow horizontally or arch downwards, growing 1 m high and covering an area of approximately 1 m². Ask at the nurseries for plants with a spreading habit or take cuttings from suitable subjects. Prune out any vertical stems to encourage lateral growth. Less vigorous than the green-leafed magenta flowered varieties, they are excellent container subjects. They also look very effective tumbling down a slope.

Bougainvillea - Shrub and container plants

Choose branched compact varieties. Many nurseries will have a large parent plant which they take cuttings from so you can check the form before you buy a plant. 'Pink Pixie' is a small leafed variety with bracts all along its branches, slow growing but with long lasting bracts, excellent for containers as is another small leafed type with pale lilac bracts.

Bougainvillea - Walls and pergolas

Look for vigorous plants making strong vertical growth, usually green leafed. There are a variety of bract colours; deep magenta, pink, yellow, orange and white. These vigorous types can easily grow more than 3 m in a year in the right conditions. These are not suitable for container cultivation as they produce stiff arching un-branched stems. Ideal however for tying to walls or growing through trees where their spines help them to wedge in the branches of the host tree.

How to achieve repeat flowering

The coloured bracts are formed on the new growth so the plant needs to be growing well. Water regularly and feed with a balanced or high nitrogen fertilizer every two weeks, switching occasionally to a high potash and phosphate fertilizer (as for tomatoes) until new growth is well established. When the new bracts begin to form, stop feeding and if possible reduce the amount of water. Enjoy the flower show until the bracts begin to fade, prune if necessary and start feeding again. In this way the plant will flower successively throughout the year.

Propagate from hard wood or semi-ripe wood cuttings, best time being the spring and autumn. The most vigorous plants root most easily while some of the more delicate slower growing varieties need more care. The roots of Bougainvillea are exceptionally brittle and often do not form a tight root ball. So, when transplanting be careful not to let the root zone crumble as this often snaps off the roots, killing the plant.

Caesalpinia pulcherrima - Peacock Flower, Dwarf Poinciana

A fast growing bush reaching 2 m. The leaves are made up of small leaflets on slender branches. The profuse flowers are produced on the branch tips and are most commonly orange, but both yellow and cerise red forms are available.

An undemanding shrub which does well on a variety of soil types; medium salt tolerance. Plant in full sun. Plants allowed to grow freely will produce some flowers continuously but the bushes tend to become straggly. Alternatively, prune the entire bush and the new growth will produce a flush of flowers. Once the flowers start to fade prune again for a fresh crop of flowers. Propagate from seed or cuttings. Flowers are produced quickly on very small plants.

WARNING: Seeds are poisonous.

Calotropis procera – Giant Milkweed
Arabic names - Oman: Shakhr, UAE: Ashuur

Native

Native to the region and the warm parts world-wide where it is often considered a weed. Its a very vigorous bush and occasionally grows into a small tree. The bush reaches approximately 3 m but can be kept neat by pruning. The leaves are grey-green and have a furry feel. The flowers which are an attractive purple and white are mainly seen in the winter months but there are some in the summer. The plant makes abundant seed on long feathery attachments which are dispersed by wind. When cut, the stem oozes white latex **which is poisonous and can give a skin reaction**. It is the favorite food of the Plain Tiger butterfly and the caterpillars can seriously reduce a plant but it quickly grows back and the caterpillars and butterflies are lovely to watch.

Grow from seed which germinate best in light, so just press the seed into the soil. Germinates 20-30°C in 5-10 days. Or look out for a seedling on a construction site where the plant is going to be destroyed. Does best in full sun with minimal water and no fertilizer. Very useful as a temporary shade plant in a new garden, providing quick shade to allow more delicate plants to establish. Use permanently where nothing else will grow. It is a butterfly magnet and the black bees come for the nectar.

Canna Indica – Canna Lily, Indian Shot

Fast growing plant with broad leaves unfurling from the centre of the clump, reaching 1.5–2 m depending on the variety. Leaves are plain green, red or striped green and yellow. Flower colours are mainly shades of yellow, orange and red and new varieties have cream, shades of pink and apricot flowers with more variation of leaf colour.

Grown in full sun or dappled shade. Though Canna can be grown on sandy soils they need at least 30 cm depth of soil and regular feeding with high nitrogen fertilizer to really flourish. Avoid competition from tree roots.

Propagation: to ensure the same characteristics as the parent plants divide up the rhizomes (underground fleshy stems which grow roots and leaves) from big clumps. Cannas can also be grown quickly from seed which might be useful for filling up a new garden. The plants from home collected seed, however, will usually be green leafed with orange to red flower colour. The seeds are very hard little balls, hence the name 'Indian Shot'. Though they will germinate eventually by soaking it is much more reliable to chip the seed coat first, then soak the seed until the root starts to show, 3-10 days at 20-30°C. Plant the seed root down just below the surface. The shoots will emerge a few days later.

Carissa macrocarpa. Syn. *C. grandiflora* - **Natal Plum**

Normally grows to a large bush reaching over 2 m with shiny dark green leathery leaves. It is often clipped to make a strong dense hedge which is supposed to be camel resistant. Lovely five-petal white fragrant flowers are produced throughout the year. The fruit is red-mauve, similar to a small plum and edible. It is often used as a hedging plant. There are also several low growing varieties such as 'Green Carpet' or 'Prostrata'. These grow to about 40 cm with horizontal spreading branches. The dwarf forms make a dense ground cover.

Plant in full sun, moderately drought tolerant, low salt tolerance. Propagate from cuttings to maintain the characteristics of the variety.

Clerodendrum inerme - **Wild Jasmine, Indian Privet**

Fast growing evergreen bush with small green leaves reminiscent of European privet. The white flowers are produced throughout the winter months and are fragrant with long protruding stamens. It is frequently trimmed to a hedge but if left it produces an exuberant, rambling, wide spreading bush.

Full sun or semi-shade. Survives high levels of soil salinity and drought but the plants look poor and unattractive with few flowers. Best in a well fertilized and irrigated site. Propagate from cuttings.

Dombeya elegans - Kenyan Wedding Flower

Large bush, fast growing and will exceed 2 m in two years. Light green large angular leaves. Spectacular rose shaped clusters of pale pink flowers in spring which darken to deep pink with age.

Enjoys full sun and looks fresh and green throughout the summer. Good wind and drought resistance. There is rapid new growth after damage from salt-laden or cold winds. Easily propagated from cuttings.

Duranta erecta - Golden Dew Drop, Sky Flower, Pigeon Berry

Sprawling bush reaching 1.2 m with a similar spread in the region. It has attractive foliage of light green, yellow or variegated leaves and clusters of pale to very dark purple flowers depending on the variety. The flowers are followed by bunches of very attractive golden berries **which are very poisonous**.

Grows well in the winter months and flowers profusely but can lose its leaves in high summer temperatures and look straggly. Trim as a hedge or keep pinching out the growing tips to encourage the plant to be bushy. Good container plant and can also be trained on to a wall. Attracts butterflies and birds but should not be planted where it would be accessible to small children.

Propagate by cuttings to keep the characteristics of the parent plant, seed would produce variable plants.

Hibiscus rosa-sinensis - Hibiscus

Perhaps the best known tropical flowering shrub. Back in the 90s every garden, park and public building had multiple different Hibiscus bushes but in early 2000 mealy bug spread throughout the region devastating all but the most resistant plants. *See Pests and Diseases section.* Bushes with single simple flowers seem to be most resistant to this pest. The most common is the bright red form but white, pink, apricot and orange flowered bushes are also available. Each flower only lasts a day but a succession of flowers ensures a plentiful supply through the winter months. In the summer the flowers are still produced but often wither before opening.

Prefers rich soil but grows well on sand as long as it is regularly fertilized with a balanced feed. An excellent container plant. Easily propagates from cuttings and starts to flower on a very small plant.

Ixora coccinea - Ixora

Several sizes are available; a large-leafed variety where the leaves are 15 cm long and can reach 2 m with a similar spread. The more compact form has smaller often rounded leaves and reaches approximately 90 cm. There is also a miniature variety. Flower colours can be white, shades of pink, peach, apricot, orange and red.

Grow in fertile, compost rich soil or regularly fertilize sandy soils. Ixoras prefer slightly acid soils. As much of the regional bedrock is alkaline it is important to add compost and fertilizer which will help make the soil acidic. Best with some shade in summer. Propagate from cuttings.

Jatropha integerrima - **Coral Plant**

Slender, often straggly shrub with large palmate dark green leaves, reaching 3 m. The bright red flowers form in clusters at the branch tips. They are produced continuously, even during the summer months. A pink-flowered variety is also available.

Single plants often look straggly, with bare woody stems with a tuft of leaves and flowers on the branch tips. Prune frequently to encourage bushy growth or plant several in a clump to produce a denser bush. Alternatively use at the back of a border where the lower plant stems can be concealed.

Easy to grow on a wide variety of soil conditions and flowers best in full sun. Low salt tolerance. Propagate from cuttings.

Lantana camara - **Shrub Verbena, Common Lantana**

A very vigorous bushy shrub reaching 2 m. The leaves are small and hairy which when crushed produce a strong aromatic smell which some people think is unpleasant. The thin angular branches are erect and slightly prickly. The flowers form in clusters on the branch tips and can be yellow and pink, reds and orange. The green berries ripen to blue black and **are poisonous**.

An undemanding plant. Plant in full sun. Drought tolerant but low salt tolerance. Does well even in poor soils. Propagates very easily from cuttings or seed and flowers quickly. Look for self-sown seedlings round a mature bush. It can be affected by mealy bug; the common yellow-pink flowered variety seems to be most resistant.

Leucophyllum frutescens - Texas Sage

Naturally rounded bush with dense green or silver-grey foliage. The flowers are variable in colour, and range between lavender and pink and are borne on the branch tips. Flowers are produced on new growth on trimmed specimens after pruning, otherwise sporadically throughout the year. Can reach 2 m with a similar spread.

Native to a limestone area of Texas and hence does well on alkaline soils in the region. Requires minimal water and do not fertilize as this produces open lax growth and fewer flowers. This is a very tough, drought and salt tolerant plant. Grow in full sun. Propagate by cuttings.

Murraya paniculata. Syn. *Murraya exotica* - **Murraya**

A dense bushy shrub up to 3 m tall and with a similar spread. The new leaves are a bright fresh green. The glossy mature dark green leaves make an attractive background for the clusters of waxy white flowers. The flowers are very fragrant and allegedly can be smelt up to 5 km from the shrub. Some people find the scent overpowering. The flowers are followed by orange-red berries.

Fast growing, making a substantial bush in a year from a cutting. Tough and easy to grow, does well on sandy soils. Grow in full sun. Propagation by cuttings or seed. The flesh must be removed from the seed and planted immediately for best germination.

Nerium oleander - Common or Pink Oleander; Arabic name: Haban

Native

A fast growing large evergreen shrub reaching up to 4 m with the same spread. The leaves are leathery, long and narrow. A very widely grown plant with the single flowered pale pink form seen growing wild in wadis. Cultivated single and double flower forms are available with a wide colour range; dark pink, pink, salmon and white. There is also a variegated leaf form with rich pink flowers. Flowers are produced continuously in clusters at the branch tips.

Well adapted to regional conditions, it thrives in full sun and is highly drought and salt tolerant. Prune severely every spring to keep the plant a reasonable size and shape. Cut a few main stems out of the centre and pull off the outer suckers, leaving a few to thicken up the base which can become rather sparse in older plants. Strikes easily from cuttings and the new plants flower in 3-4 months.

WARNING: All parts of this plant are highly poisonous. Don't even use as firewood as the smoke can be irritating. Wash your hands after handling.

Nyctanthes arbor-tristis – Tree of Sorrow

A must for every garden, the fragrance in the evening is fantastic even from a few flowers. A stiff branched shrub with rough, slightly hairy leaves and white and egg yolk yellow small tubular flowers. The flowers come out at dusk and drop the next morning, scattering the ground with spent blooms like teardrops, hence the sorrowful name. In ideal conditions can reach 10 m but 2-3 m is more common. An excellent pot subject as it flowers on a very small shrub. Easily propagated by cuttings or the large two-lobed seed. Remove the developing seed to extend flowering. Flowers through the winter.

Plumbago auriculata. Syn. *P. capensis* - **Cape Plumbago**

A rambling, trailing bush making an arching mound. Or it can be trained against a trellis. The small leaves are light green. During the winter months it is smothered with lovely powder blue flowers. Trim off the spent flowers to encourage a second flush.

Plant in the autumn to get the plant well established before the summer as it is susceptible to leaf burn possibly killing newly planted plants. Plant in dappled shade or provide shade over the summer months. Excellent as a container plant which can be moved into the shade over the summer. Low salt and drought tolerance. Propagate from green cuttings.

Plumeria species – Frangipani

Plumeria obtusa

An evergreen tall open shrub or small tree reaching approximately 4 m. The long leather green leaves have a very rounded tip. The flowers are sweetly fragrant and mainly white.

Plumeria rubra

Is deciduous, losing all its leaves in the winter months. The leaves are a slightly lighter green and have a pointed tip. The flowers are fragrant and range in colour from dark pink through pale pink, cream or white with a yellow throat.

Both species are inclined to grow in a lax open manner with contorted branches at odd angles. The new branches, however, are quite flexible so can be trained along sticks to make a pleasing shape. Good in a large pot as a bush, or in open ground can be grown as a screen.

Easy to grow, does well in full sun and is drought tolerant. Grows on a wide range of soil types but has low salt tolerance. Propagate from cuttings, allow the white sap to dry on the end of the cutting before placing it in the soil in a shady spot. Do not cover with plastic and keep the soil just moist.

Tabernaemontana divaricata - **Pinwheel Bush**

Very neat naturally symmetrical bush with lovely shiny leaves which set off the five-petaled white flowers. The flowers are shaped like a child's pinwheel and swirl round the central point. Not usually fragrant in the region as apparently the scent is vaporized by sunshine and high temperatures. Can reach up to 3 m but can be pruned to size. There is also a double-flowered hybrid plant, probably 'Flore Pleno'.

Grows moderately quickly on sandy soils and is drought tolerant. Grows rapidly and looks better with regular applications of fertilizer. Does best and flowers most freely in full sun, tends to be less dense in partial shade. Good pot subject as it flowers on a small plant.

Tecoma stans - **Yellow Trumpet Flower**

Large bush or multi-stemmed tree of up to 5 m. Its bright green foliage is made up of five saw tooth-edged fingers. During the winter months it flowers repeatedly and bushes are often smothered with clusters of cheerful yellow flowers. *Tecoma alata* is orange-flowered, less vigorous with darker small leaves.

After flowering prune back shoots giving new growth which will flower again in 5-8 weeks. The seeds are produced in bean-like pods and if allowed to ripen, the plant will not flower again until these have dispersed. Over time the bushes can become tall and straggly but can be pruned back to 45 cm or so and will regenerate.

Does well in full sun even on exposed windy sites. Moderate salt and drought tolerance. Seed is plentiful but germinates slowly, so plants are usually produced from cuttings.

Thevetia peruviana - Yellow Oleander

Narrow leafed bush reaching 4 m with cream, apricot or, more commonly, yellow flowers. Flowers continuously throughout the year though less in summer. It produces cubed small green fruits which turn black with time and are said to look like Chinese 'lucky nuts'

A very reliable plant which thrives in full sun, does well in sandy and alkaline soils, is drought tolerant and has a high salt tolerance. Propagate from cuttings or seed, remove the fleshy fruit from around the nut before planting.

WARNING: Seeds and flowers are poisonous and cause an erratic heartbeat. Wash hands after handling.

Thunbergia erecta - Bush Thunbergia, Kings Mantle

Grown for its rich purple flowers with yellow throats produced abundantly throughout the winter months. There is also a white flowered form which is less striking. A rambling arching shrub which makes a spindly bush of about 1 m². It looks better trimmed as a hedge where the small leaves make it a good subject. While it is being established there will be few flowers due to the constant trimming.

This is a delicate plant under regional conditions as it burns and looks poor in the summer heat. It recovers into vigorous life in the winter. Does well on sandy soils with regular fertilizer in the winter months. Good in partial shade or a pot which can be moved to the shade in the summer. Propagate by cuttings which strike easily.

Vitex agnus-castus - Arabian Lilac. Arabic name: Arshad

Vigorous plant reaching more than 5 m with a similar spread. The lanceolate leaves are dark green on top and silver underneath and have a fruity smell when crushed. Some branches produce variegated leaves of green and white. Masses of blue-mauve flower spikes are borne on the stem tips in spring and autumn attracting birds, bees and butterflies.

Very tough, fast growing and thrives in full sun. High salt tolerance and can withstand salt laden winds. Drought tolerant, but will lose its leaves under extreme conditions. Tends to become rather straggly. Prune back hard to maintain a good shape. Even a thick stem can be pruned and will generate new leaves from the base. Propagate from hard wood cuttings which strike easily.

CLIMBERS, & TWINERS

Tropical climbers are exciting plants to grow. Their prodigious growth rate and spectacular flushes of flowers make them a must. In small courtyards and balconies using vertical space increases the growing area and adds interest. Grown over a pergola or trellis climbers provide delightful dappled shade and bring interest and life to otherwise stark walls.

Choosing climbers

Before selecting climbing plants consider what you want to achieve, dense shade, hiding an ugly wall, vertical interest in a limited space; this will dictate the plant you choose. Many climbers are really vigorous; Coral Vine, *Antigonon* and Yellow Mandevilla, *Urechites* reach 3 m in height in their first year with a similar spread. Others have more modest growth, such as *Allamanda*, either the yellow flowered *A. cathartica* or purple flowered *A.violacea*, and respond well to being pruned to keep them neat and compact so the flowers are produced at eye level.

Planting

Prepare the soil as for shrubs with fertilizer and compost. It is essential to feed climbers generously to allow them to sustain rapid growth, which can be 3-4 m in the first year.

Climbers can be divided into three groups: Self-clinging, Scandent and Twining.

Self-clinging such as the Orange Trumpet Flower, *Campsis* has tufts of short adventitious rootlets along its stems which are designed to cling onto surfaces. Though the roots don't penetrate the wall their grip is very strong and will often pull off paint and loose plaster if they are pulled off.

Scandent; these are scrambling, rambling or trailing plants. These plants produce long arching stems which naturally lie on top of structures or other plants. Some have curved thorns to help them cling on, such as Bougainvillea, but if they are to be grown on a vertical surface they need to be tied on to strong supports.

Twining plants twine round any support available; wire trellis or other plants. In some cases the whole stem twines round, such as Rangoon Creeper, *Quisqualis*. Others have specially adapted tendrils which are able to cling on to narrow supports, such as wire, but struggle to cling on to thick trellis e.g. the Coral Vine, *Antigonon*.

Supports

A wooden trellis makes good support for climbers. Mount the trellis so it is slightly away from the wall allowing stems to be woven through or tied on to the front. Alternatively hammer in concrete nails into the wall and stretch wire between them. Tie the plant to the wire so it is away from the wall allowing a cool air space behind it as walls get exceedingly hot in summer. Wire can also be stretched vertically from ground to roof level of house walls allowing twining stems to make a flowery column. Use strong, stretchy ties to tie plants to the support which don't damage the plant as it thickens; old nylon tights are a good option.

Pruning

The aim of pruning is to produce a pleasing shape and a healthy plant by cutting out dead wood and over-crowded branches. Most climbers naturally grow vertically resulting in a tall thin plant with all the leaves and flowers up above. To avoid this pinch out the vertical tips or cut back vertical stems to lateral branches and train these sideways. If you inherit a climber which is all woody stems below cut back two-thirds of the branches to the last bud above ground level. Feed well and wait until strong new growth appears on the cut branches before cutting the remaining long branches. Main pruning should be done prior to a growing season, either in late summer or early spring, while light pruning can be carried out as necessary.

Allamanda species - Trumpet Vine

Allamandas do best in sheltered, slightly shaded sites as drought resistance is poor. Salt tolerance is low. They prefer neutral soil, keep it well fertilized and mulch with compost round the base to avoid soils becoming alkaline which can result in the plant failing to thrive and showing signs of chlorosis. Propagate from cuttings. **The milky sap is a skin irritant**.

Allamanda cathartica – Golden Trumpet Vine

A woody climber or rambling shrub reaching 3-5 m. It has glossy green leaves and bright yellow trumpet shaped flowers. The flowers are borne on the branch tips throughout the year but with a flush of flowers in autumn and spring.

Allamanda violacea. Syn. *A. blanchetii* - Purple Trumpet Vine

Has dark red-brown buds followed by rich purple trumpet flowers in clusters on the branch tips. A well known cultivar 'Cherry Jubilee' has darker larger flowers. The leaves are rounded and quite hairy especially on the underside. The arching stems can be tied onto a trellis or cut down every year to form a bush. Pinching out the tips of the new growth encourages the stems to branch resulting in more flowers in spring and autumn.

Antigonon leptopus - Coral Vine

A quick growing climber reaching 10-12 m. It has bunches of frothy coral pink flowers in the winter months and sparser flowers midwinter and summer. Tendrils make it self-supporting but it needs to be tied to smooth surfaces. Alternatively it will trail down slopes or make a rambling ground cover plant.

Thrives in full sun in a sheltered location away from strong winds. Drought and salt tolerance low. Best in rich soil with high organic content to provide plenty of nutrient for its prodigious growth. Propagate from stem or root cuttings.

Bougainvillea

Choose vigorous, naturally erect types for training over walls and pergolas. These are usually the dark red-purple 'flowered' types. On smooth surfaces the stems need to be tied in but through trees the Bougainvillea hooks will be sufficient support. *For full cultivation notes refer to the Shrub Section.*

Campsis - Orange Trumpet Flower

A rampant self-supporting climber using especially adapted aerial root suckers. Even on concrete walls it can reach phenomenal heights, easily covering a four-story building. The clusters of tubular orange flowers are produced all through the summer. It is semi-deciduous during the winter months in exposed sites and the stems can look dead and lifeless until late spring.

Really thrives in full sun and does best in rich fertile soil where its growth rate is prodigious. Can be grown in a pot for a few years but in the long term it needs an open site. Low salt tolerance, some drought resistance. Despite the clinging roots, cuttings seem to have poor success. Propagate by layering, or by taking almost ripe wood cuttings in the summer. Alternatively take pencil thick 5 cm plus root cuttings in the winter. In some locations the vine produces viable seed.

Clitoria ternatea - Butterfly Pea, Blue Pea Flower

A vigorous bushy climber with bright blue flowers which have a white throat. Flowers well over the winter months but has some flowers throughout the year. The slender stems twine quickly over fences or plants and the leaves are rounded mid green.

Does well in a wide range of soils including alkaline conditions. Low salt and drought tolerance. It is drought deciduous and needs regular irrigation to prevent dead patches appearing on the vine. After a few years it produces a tangled mess. Prune two-thirds back to near ground level, feed and once new growth has started prune back the rest. Propagation by seed or cuttings. Soak seeds overnight then germination takes 7-10 days at 20-30°C. Plants bloom in 7-10 weeks. Like most pea type plants the roots fix nitrogen and so improve soil fertility. It can also be grown as green manure (see soils). Successful as a container plant.

Ipomoea palmata - **Railway Creeper**

Fast growing twining creeper reaching over 10 m. It has distinctive five or seven lobed leaves. The purple bell-shaped flowers are short lived but plentiful during the winter months. Flowering is much diminished in the summer.

A hardy plant growing well even in poor soils. Drought tolerant though under extreme conditions, it will die back to its roots sprouting again when conditions moderate. Tolerant of salt winds. Though it is used as a ground cover it is an enthusiastic climber and requires a lot of effort to keep it off other plants and trees. Propagate from cuttings.

Jacquemontia pentantha - **Blue Flowered Creeper**

A rampant slender stemmed twining vine which quickly forms a mass of stems. The small sky blue cone shaped flowers have a white centre and are borne in profusion all winter. The leaves are heart shaped mid-green colour.

Requires plenty of moisture and retentive organic material to prevent it wilting in the summer heat. Low salt and drought tolerance. Propagate by taking plenty of stem cuttings which will root in water. When the rooted cuttings are transplanted to soil cover with a plastic bag and place in a shady place until the plants start to produce new leaves. Alternatively plant seeds. The seeds are tiny, so shake a handful of flowering stems over a seed tray or look for self sown seedlings. Can be grown as a container plant but start with a large pot as it needs a good moisture reservoir.

Jasminum species

Jasminum grandiflorum - Spanish Jasmine

The stems are rather stiff and arching and need to be tied into a support. The leaves are very dark green and usually divided into seven slender leaflets. The large flowers are 4 cm across, white tinged with mauve underneath and have a sweet fragrance. The main flowering period is spring but there is a second flush of flowers in autumn.

Jasminum fluminense, subspecies gratissimum - Arabian Jasmine; often called Jasminum officinale in the region, Common Jasmine

The stems are slender and flexible, twining round supports or other plants. The leaves are made up of three ovate leaflets. Widely grown in the region for its very fragrant small pure white flowers, 3 cm across borne in clusters. Main flowering time is late spring into early summer but with a scattering of flowers over the summer.

Both species are drought tolerant but can look poor in the high summer, however, they recover in the autumn. Prune out damaged and unsightly branches at the end of the summer to regenerate nice fresh looking new growth. Low salt tolerance. Propagate from cuttings or from the small black fruits which are attractive to the birds. Look for self-sown seedlings. Transplants are often slow to establish but produce rapid growth thereafter. Prune to shape at the end of the summer. Jasminum fluminense is a successful pot subject, either grown up a support or allowed to ramble over the edge of the pot.

Quisqualis indica - **Rangoon Creeper**

A very vigorous woody climber it is frequently seen twining up vertical wires against house walls where it can climb 20 m. Second only to Bougainvillea for masses of flowers in the spring and autumn. The whole vine is covered with clusters of pink and white tubular flowers which darken to red with age and exude a sweet fragrance. There is also a double flowered form which grows more slowly, making it a better subject for a pot or limited space.

Thrives in full sun. Best in rich soil and with regular feeding to sustain its prodigious growth. Semi deciduous in winter depending on how exposed the site is. Prune out dead stems to keep the plant tidy. Pinch out the stem tips frequently on new plants to encourage more stems at the base. Propagation; the easiest method is to sever runners produced by mature plants. Cut through the root linking the new plant to the parent plant making sure the new plant has plenty of roots. Pot it up separately and grow it on carefully until it is fully established and can be planted out. Cuttings are considered difficult.

Single

Double

Urechites lutea - **Yellow Mandevilla, Wild Allamander**

A very vigorous climber with twining stems reaching 8-10 m in a year. Bright yellow cone shaped flowers, 5-7 cm long are borne on the stem tips enhanced by bright green shiny leaves. Main flowering time is late spring with a second flush of flowers in the autumn and a few flowers throughout the year. A versatile plant, it can also be grown as a rambling shrub, trailed over a wall or even as ground cover if kept well trimmed. Tolerates full sun but the leaves look bleached by midsummer and is better with some shade. Looks wonderful grown together with the equally vigorous *Jacquemontia pentantha*, Blue Flowered Creeper, as shown at the start of this section.

Tolerant of a wide range of soils including alkaline and poor sands. It is highly drought tolerant and has moderate salt tolerance. The leaves seem to be resistant to salty winds so does well by the coast. It can be grown in a pot for a year or two if well fed and watered but long term needs to be in open ground to thrive. **All parts of the plant are poisonous** and the milk white sap may cause skin irritation. Propagate by soft or hard wood cuttings.

TREES

Trees are a wonderful addition to any landscape, softening new buildings, providing shade and a home for a variety of fauna. In particular the native tree species *Boswellia*, *Moringa peregina*, *Prosopis cineraria*, and *Ziziphus* contribute habitat for indigenous species. In addition they are ideally suited to the environment being drought, salt and alkaline tolerant. Native trees have a reputation for being slow growing but under garden conditions they produce a slender tree in 1-2 years and a substantial specimen in five years. Contribute to the environment by planting a native tree!

The best time to plant trees is autumn so that they are well established before the summer heat. When choosing a tree it is important to consider its eventual size and root and shade density. To get a really good idea check in local parks and other people's gardens to see what shape and size the tree is eventually going to be. Due to the climate and frequently poor soils many trees do not reach their full potential and the same species is smaller than in other parts of the world.

Propagation

Most trees are grown from seed. Their thick tough seed coats often need to be 'scarified' or nicked to allow water to penetrate the seed and encourage rapid germination. *See Plant Propagation.*

Native trees are not commonly available from nurseries but germinate readily from seed. Plant some extra and offer them to school projects as there is an increasing interest in native plants and the environment.

Acacia nilotica, subspecies *indica* - Babul, Prickly Acacia
Arabic name: Qarat.

A medium-sized tree reaching 4-8 m with a rounded crown and a dense network of branches when mature. There is a long flowering period, all through the cooler months trees are covered with round fluffy yellow flowers which are faintly scented and very attractive to bees. The flowers are followed by plentiful, pale green 'ziz-zag' shaped pods turning light brown as they dry out.

Originally from Pakistan and India it thrives in the region but does not usually self-seed without some additional assistance. Once established it survives with minimal additional water. Initially the trees are very thorny but this reduces as the tree matures. Fast growing, producing a three-metre slender tree in 2-3 years. Deep rooted, which helps make it drought resistant. Nitrogen-fixing nodules on the roots aid its growth on poor soils.

Easily raised from fresh seed, soak the seed overnight and then plant half buried in the soil. Germination 3-5 days at 20-30°C. May be difficult to find in nurseries.

Albizia lebbeck - Mother's Tongue, Rain Tree

A large 12-15 m tall tree in the region with an equal spread. The dense dark green foliage is made up of bi-pinnate leaves. The early summer flowers are produced in abundance covering the tree with very pale yellow fluffy balls. The flowers are fragrant at night. These are followed by large flat pods which stay on the tree until the next pods are produced and rattle audibly in the breeze. Later in the summer, leaf loss can make the tree look rather desiccated and unattractive.

An easily cultivated tree with medium salt tolerance and drought resistant. Though generally wind resistant, after a storm the ground is scattered with small twigs. Germinates easily from seed as the abundance of self-sown seedlings demonstrate.

Azadirachta indica - Neem Tree

A lush looking tree with dense foliage in a large rounded crown which looks fresh and green even during the summer months. Reaches 10 m in height. The new leaves are bright green, darkening with maturity. Each leaf is made up of 7-9 pairs of leaflets. These are elongated with serrated edges and more dense at the branch ends. In spring the clusters of small fragrant flowers cover the tree giving it a white appearance and are attractive to bees. The olive-sized fruits are green turning black with maturity.

A fast growing vigorous tree, expect a sapling to double its size in six months. The tree produces a very dense canopy which produces deep shade. The lateral roots are thick and fibrous so together with the shade nothing can be grown underneath.

A very reliable tough tree which is notably drought and moderately salt tolerant. Propagates easily from fresh seed. Remove the flesh from the seed and plant, germination 14-21 days at 20-30°C. Can be susceptible to scaly bug and sooty mould which can damage young trees

Bauhinia purpurea - Purple Orchid or Butterfly Tree

A very graceful small tree reaching 6 m with a similar spread. Moderately fast growing, reaching over 2 m height and spread in four years. The leaves are grey green and bi-lobed. Spectacular pink-purple orchid-like flowers, 10 cm across, are produced on the new growth in spring and autumn. They are followed by flat green pods which darken with age. The branches droop slightly making an excellent shade tree. Deciduous or semi-deciduous during the winter months.

Prefers a well cultivated site and does better with some shading from the afternoon sun. Has low salt tolerance and requires regular irrigation. Leaves fold together at night and under stress. Propagate from seed which germinates easily. Seed grown plants usually flower after three years.

Boswellia sacra – Frankincense. Arabic name: Luban Native

Renowned worldwide for its production of Frankincense this native of Dohfar (Southern Oman) grows well throughout the region. This small tree tends to be multi-stemmed with stiff upright branches. It is semi-deciduous depending on the how exposed the site is, losing its leaves in late winter followed immediately by new growth. The yellow white-scented flowers are produced in early spring followed by round seed pods. In the wild the trees are usually 2-3 metres but under garden cultivation can be taller. The peeling bark can be scraped back to produce the delicious frankincense smell.

Does well in the region, tolerating a wide variety of soils including very rocky limestone locations and makes an interesting specimen in a pot. Propagate by cuttings and though the tree does produce viable seed it is difficult to germinate.

Callistemon species - Bottlebrush

Evergreen shrub or small tree. It is characterized by narrow stemless leaves and brilliant red cylindrical flowers. The flowers are clustered together around the branch tips and look like bottle brushes. The main flowering period is spring with a second flush of flowers in autumn. There are two species commonly grown in the region.

Both species are hardy, resistant to drought and wind but have very low salt tolerance and are relatively slow growing.

C. citrinus - Lemon Bottlebrush

This is the smaller of the two reaching 1-3 m. It can be grown as a dense shrub or multi-stemmed tree. New foliage is orange-green in spring followed by a flush of flowers of intense red.

C. viminalis - Weeping Bottlebrush

As its name suggests it has arching pendulous branches and leaves with a more pointed tip. The tree reaches 5 m and makes an impressive sight in spring covered with flowers.

Propagate from soft wood cuttings. Plants grown from seed have a wide variation in shape and habit and take a long time before they are a sizeable plant.

Cassia species

Cassia fistula - Indian Laburnum, Golden Shower Tree

A tall slender tree reaching 8 -10 m. Trees partly lose their foliage during the winter months and in spring produce first flowers and then new foliage. The attractive light green foliage is made up of pairs of ovate leaflets which form each slender leaf. The masses of yellow flowers are borne in long pendulous clusters up to 80 cm long and are a spectacular sight for several weeks. The long dark pods contain a sweet pulp which has a laxative effect.

Fast growing, reaching 2 m in the first year, though it doesn't usually flower until the third year. Not a very robust tree in the region, needing protection from wind, salt free irrigation and humus rich soil. It's worth the effort, however, for the magnificent flowers. Propagate from seed, but scarify and soak for 24 hours before sowing or germination can take a year.

Flowers are produced first, on bare wood (right), followed by leaves (above)

Cassia siamea. Syn. *Senna siamea* - **Yellow Cassia**

Fast growing, small tree reaching approximately 5 metres. Bipinnate mid green leaves which stay attractive and green even during the summer months. The crown is dense and spreading making this a good shade tree. The yellow flowers are produced in spring and autumn, followed by long black, brown pods.

A robust tree, grows well on well drained sandy soils and can tolerate alkaline conditions. Propagate from fresh seed, older seed may require scarifying.

Casuarina equisetifolia - **Australian Pine, Horsetail Tree, She-oak**

Looks like a conifer at first glance with grey-green, finely much divided branches. The leaves are reduced to tiny scales arranged in whorls. Small round cones contain winged seeds. A fast growing tree reaching 15 m at maturity, it will grow 4 m in four years in good growing conditions. There is a huge variation between individuals in the shape and look of the tree. Some are much neater and denser than others which have a very open ragged appearance. *Casuarina* can be pruned into a dense bush or other topiary forms.

A tough tree growing where other trees would fail, it is drought tolerant with minimal irrigation requirements. Over-watering causes soft fast growth which makes it vulnerable to storm damage. It has a very high salt tolerance and will withstand salt laden winds so is often used in coastal sites. Propagate from seed though the resulting individuals vary considerably in shape and form.

Conocarpus lancifolius - Kuwaiti Tree

Not suitable for anything but a very large garden.

A tall bushy tree, super fast growing, reaching over 4 m in the first year once established. Slender leaves borne in clusters. The tree thickens out naturally at 3-4 m into a very attractive shape. Fluffy yellow-green flowers are borne in clusters in spring and autumn which have a strong unpleasant smell at night. These are followed by small green berry fruits containing small seeds. Introduced into Kuwait on a large scale, hence the common name, but it is a native of Florida Keys and the Everglades.

A great tree to use as a wind break on exposed sites. Very tough high salt tolerance. The roots below are as dense and wide spreading as the branches above and soon completely dominate the surrounding area preventing anything else from growing. It is often used as a pioneer plant to stabilize sand. Sometimes grown in pots but the growth tends to be sparse, unlike the dense leafy green of even small plants in the open ground.

Propagates easily from semi ripe wood cuttings. Germination from seed is poor, less than 15%. New research suggests the seed should be germinated in water with a layer of soil below. Once the roots start to appear the water should be allowed to evaporate letting the roots hook into the soil. The seedlings are then grown on in the normal way.

Cordia sebestena - Scarlet Cordia, Geiger Tree

A neat small tree reaching 3-5 m, with large rounded leaves. Beautiful, brilliant orange flowers are borne in clusters over a long period, so fruits and flowers are on the tree together. The edible fruits are white, oval and sweet with a large stone.

Does well on a wide range of soil types and is moderately drought tolerant. Successfully grown as a roadside tree but produces a much denser rounded head in association with other trees or in lawns. Salt tolerance moderate. Propagate from seed which germinates in 14-21 days.

Delonix regia - Royal Poinciana, Flame of the Forest

A magnificent tree smothered in vivid red orange flowers in early summer. Medium sized reaching 5 m in the region with a wide spreading crown of dark green feathery foliage. Moderate growth rate and usually flowers after 2-3 years. It is semi-deciduous, losing most of its foliage at the end of winter, prior to flowering. The flowers are initially produced on bare branches making the display even more stunning. The thick flat dark pods grow up to 45 cm long.

Prefers well-drained soils and enjoys the higher humidity of a coastal area but away from direct salt winds. It has spreading shallow roots making it difficult to grow anything underneath. Its brittle branches are often damaged by high winds giving rise to dead sections in the canopy. Its soft wood can be vulnerable to termites. Propagate from seed which must be scarified and soaked in hot water before planting.

Ficus species
Ficus benjamina - Weeping Fig

A slender tree with shiny ovate leaves and pendulous branches. Usually seen as a container tree where it can reach 3 m despite the cramped conditions. As a garden plant it needs a sheltered site but can mature into a large spreading tree. The small berry fruits are yellow or red. The variety 'nuda' has smaller leaves and a more erect habit. In addition there are five or six variegated varieties. These are less vigorous and suitable for containers in a shady patio garden or indoors.

Drought tolerant and prefers well drained sandy soils but benefits from some summer shading.

Ficus microcarpa - Laurel Fig

A very versatile tree with dense shiny green leaves. The trunk is a lovely smooth light silver grey which sets off the foliage. There are two forms; one which has an upright very bushy habit is ideal for clipping into multiple formal shapes, possibly *F. microcarpa* var. *nitida* and another which has a slightly weeping habit and is best used as a specimen tree. Either can be grown in a container to a substantial size. In the open ground they can reach 10 m.

Reasonably fast growing and producing lots of new light green shiny leaves all year except the height of summer.

A moderately hardy tree which is medium salt tolerant and drought resistant. In very hot sites the leaves burn in summer on the side of the prevailing wind. Nurseries propagate new trees from cuttings which produces a saleable plant quickly but seed also germinates easily. Self-sown seedlings are frequent.

Ficus religiosa - Sacred Bo, Bo Tree, Peepul

So called because it is sacred to both Hindus and Buddhists and is said to be the tree under which the Buddha reputedly gained enlightenment. This is a potentially large tree of over 15 m in good conditions. It is fast growing, reaching over 3 m in the first two years. The leaves are large, hand sized, initially pale pink, then green turning to dark green with maturity. Each leaf has a long pointy drip tip. The leaves rustle in the lightest wind making a characteristic sound reminiscent of Poplar.

Does best in deep rich soil where it is able to maintain rapid growth. It will however grow in a wide range of soil types and is moderately salt tolerant but growth tends to be more erratic in these conditions and the leaves are smaller. Propagate from either cuttings, which root easily, even large pieces can be successfully rooted, or fresh seed germinates easily; self-sown seedlings are common.

Leucaena leucocephala - Speedy Tree

Plant this tree with caution.

An exceptionally fast growing multi-stemmed bush or tree reaching over 8 m. The leaves are made up of small leaflets. The flowers are borne in summer and have the appearance of fluffy yellow balls with long protruding stamens. The slender brown pods which form in clusters at the branch tips are packed full of seed which germinate everywhere! Nurseries no longer consider it suitable as a garden plant.

A very hardy tree withstanding drought and high levels of salinity. It thrives in alkaline soils. It was originally planted in tropical areas to feed cattle and withstands repeated cutting back, meaning it is difficult to eradicate. Propagate by seed or collect self-sown seedlings.

Millingtonia hortensis - Cork Tree, Tree Jasmine

A slender tree with relatively few branches so it creates pleasant light dappled shade, allowing grass or other plants to grow underneath. Fast growing tree reaching 10-12 m. The dark green foliage is toothed and very divided. In spring and autumn it is smothered in clusters of beautiful dangling white tubular flowers. The flowers open in the evening and are particularly fragrant at night.

Does well in thin poor soils including highly alkaline ones. Drought and wind tolerant. It produces multiple root suckers which spread into surrounding lawns or borders. Consequently it is easily propagated from root suckers or from cuttings; even big pieces will root.

Moringa species

Moringa oleifera - Drumstick Tree, Horseradish tree

A tall graceful tree with long much divided bi-pinnate leaves giving light shade. Fast growing, reaching 10 m. In spring the tree is covered with highly scented white flowers which are followed by very long angular pods. These grow to nearly half a metre. The edible pods are often used in curries and oil can be extracted from the seeds. Moringa is now considered a very important tree in the developing world as virtually all the parts are edible and it can be used to supplement people's diets.

Does well in the region. It is medium salt and drought resistant. Propagate from seed.

Moringa peregrina - Arabic name: Shu

A native tree in Oman and the U.A.E, often seen growing high up in rocky crevices or on steep wadi sides. Trees in the wild reach only 3-4 m but under garden cultivation larger specimens are common. The branches and leaves are grey-green, thin and wispy. Profuse flowers are produced in early spring which have white petals with pink veins and are sweetly scented. These are followed by long slender pods. Like *Moringa oleifera* the seeds are rich in oil which is extracted and used in cooking and the preparation of herbal medicines.

A tree ideally suited to the regional conditions as it is highly drought tolerant and medium salt tolerant. It has great potential as a garden plant though as yet it is not widely available in nurseries. Propagated from freshly collected seed. Soak the seeds in water prior to planting. Germination takes 7-10 days. The seedlings look

nothing like the parent plant, being bushy with small round leaves sprouting from a thick white tuber. *See page 14*. As the tree matures the round leaflets die back leaving only the leaf axils giving the plant the wispy look. Initially the tree will need irrigation but once established it should survive without.

Parkinsonia aculeata - Jerusalem Thorn

A small tree or multi-stemmed shrub reaching 4-6 m with a similar spread. The slender arched branches give the tree a broad canopy. The leaves are made up of small leaflets attached to wispy branches producing light shade. In spring and autumn the tree has clusters of attractive, fragrant, sulphur-yellow flowers with orange stamens. followed by long beans. The branches are thorny so it needs to be positioned carefully. In the summer the tree is semi-deciduous in response to the high temperatures.

A well adapted tree to the regional conditions being a highly drought resistant tree with minimal irrigation requirements. Over-watering may cause it to rot. Grows on thin poor soils in alkaline conditions and next to the sea.

Propagation: nurseries prefer to use soft wood cuttings for fast production but the abundant seed germinates easily.

Peltophorum pterocarpum - Yellow Flame Tree, Yellow Poinciana

A handsome, large spreading tree reaching 10-12 m. The new foliage in spring looks a rich velvet dark green, making a lovely background for the erect candles of fragrant bright yellow flowers. A rusty coloured brown fuzz covers new growth. Dark red-black pods with four seeds per pod follow the flowers.

Low salt tolerance, best on a fertile site. Propagate from seed which needs to be chipped or sandpapered at one end or placed in boiling water for two minutes then soaked in cold water overnight. Seed grown trees take 3-4 years before they flower. As initial growth is one single vertical stem, pinch out the terminal bud to encourage side branches. Propagate from seed.

Phoenix dactylifera - Date Palm. Arabic name: Nakhl

The arching fronds of a the date palm against a blue sky must be a common image of the region. This attractive tree is highly prized for ornamental and agricultural purposes. There are approximately 150 varieties of dates grown in the region, producing 1 million metric tones of dates a year.

The date palm is a large tree, the canopy is made up of long arching lance shaped leaves up to 6 m long. The trees are either male or female and dates are only produced on a female plant which will need fertilization. Pollination is by wind but this only works where there are 50/50 male and female trees. In date plantations the ratio is usually about one male to 50-100 female trees. In a garden setting, an isolated female tree will need to be hand pollinated. Take a male flower stalk and shake the pollen over the female flowers, leave the male stalk amongst the female flowers to maximize fertilization.

Once the dates have set tie them up so they are not damaged by being buffeted against the tree. Dates take five or six months to ripen, some are nice fresh, others are better dried. Well-cultivated mature trees produce 50-150 kg of dates.

Date palms can easily be grown from seed but take up to eight years to start fruiting, assuming the tree is female. Mostly new palms are grown from suckers of female plants that fruit well; these can produce fruit in 2-3 years depending on how mature they are. As demonstrated by many newly landscaped areas mature palms can be relocated, at a cost. For the home gardener small trees can be purchased but even a tree with a one metre trunk is immensely heavy, requiring 3-4 men to transport it and plant it. Keep newly planted trees shaded and moist but not wet as this risks rotting the stem.

Tolerant of both high alkaline and saline conditions. Though it is drought tolerant it needs good irrigation or its roots in the water table to fruit well. A mature tree needs up to 120 litres of water a day in mid summer (equivalent of two cycles of an automatic washing machine).

Pithecellobium dulce - Manila Tamarind

Small dark green bi-lobed leaves make up the dense crown of this small tree, which reaches 4-6 m. It is deciduous but the new leaves appear immediately the old ones die so it appears evergreen. The branches are prickly so it requires careful sighting. Flowering takes place in spring. The creamy white fragrant flowers are followed by curled red pods containing sweet edible pink pulp and large dark seeds.

Minimal water requirements. Moderately salt tolerant. The roots have nitrogen fixing nodules enabling it to grow on poor thin soils with little or no fertilizer. Propagated from abundant seed.

Pongamia glabra - Pongamia

The long pendulous branches are covered with closely packed shiny ovate leaves, producing a dense crown. The branches will arch to touch the ground if not pruned. In spring the new growth has lovely shades of pale pink and lime green. The flowers can be white, pink or pale lilac and are produced in early summer. The flat seed pods contain a single seed. Slow growth rate reaching a maximum height of 8 m. It has a wide spread, however, making this a good shade tree.

Saline tolerant and does well near the coast but needs plentiful water either fresh or brackish. On windy exposed sites the leaves sometimes burn in summer but soon make up the loss in autumn. Propagate from seed or suckers.

Prosopis species
Prosopis cineraria - **Arabic name: Ghaf**

Native to the region it is the largest and most attractive tree in the wild. It is seen in sandy areas, gravel plains and wadi beds. Established trees can reach 12 m with a dense crown of grey-green leaves giving wonderful shade. In the past some individuals were the tallest feature in the landscape and were used as significant landmarks. The tree shape is variable, some trees have erect branches while others are pendulous giving the tree a shape reminiscent of a weeping willow. The leaves are made up of small leaflets, 7-10 pairs to each leaf. In late spring the tree is covered in fresh new green growth. This is followed by drooping pale yellow catkin-like flowers and subsequently slender pods containing small black seeds. The pods and leaves are used locally for animal feed and the flowers provide an important source of nectar for honey production.

Ideally suited to regional conditions with minimal water requirements and moderately salt tolerant. Propagate from seed, soak the seed overnight then plant shallowly. Germination takes 5-10 days at 25-30°C. The tap root is very well developed, so use a deep pot or root trainers or plant out even when the seedling is tiny. The root system is reported to reach depths of up to 35 metres and it can stabilize sand. In the wild this is a slow growing tree but under garden conditions the lead shoot can reach over two metres in the first year and be a substantial tree in four years. Initially the tree is very prickly but this reduces as the tree matures.

Prosopis juliflora - **Thorn Tree.**

A fast growing thorny tree with spreading branches which rest on the ground. The leaves are made up of finely divided leaflets and are light green when new. These darken to bottle green with maturity and produce a dense shady canopy. The dangling catkin-like flowers are pale yellow and are produced mainly in spring and a few in autumn. These are followed by long green pods, up to 25 cm long, which change to straw colour with age and are full of seed.

Do not plant this tree. It has escaped into the wild, threatening native habitat.

In many respects this is the 'Tyrannosaurus Rex' of ornamental plants grown in the region. It is able to grow where nothing else will and has escaped into the wild where it threatens natural habitats. It is exceptionally salt and drought tolerant. In gardens its roots can extend over 30 m, completely strangling every other plant and will even grow into pots standing on the soil. The thorns can puncture feet and car tires and the black sap stains clothes and furniture. The cultivation of other plants under *Prosopis juliflora* is impossible, as the leaf litter probably contains a chemical which suppresses any other seedlings. It is hard to irradicate even by repeatedly cutting back and application of weed killer. Its dense wood makes excellent camp fires.

Tabebuia heterophylla. Syn. *T. pallida* – **Pink Trumpet Tree**
Possibly hybridised with *Tabebuia rosea*

A neat tree, with long oval shaped leathery green leaves with a blunt tip, evergreen, reaching approximately 8-10 m. In early summer the tree is covered with pale delicate pink trumpet shaped flowers with a pale yellow throat which fade to white. There is a second flowering period in autumn with a few flowers sporadically throughout the year. Moderately fast growing making a 2 m tall tree in a year. Remove the lower branches to encourage height or leave them to create a bush or multi-stemmed tree. In some areas the flowers are followed by long green pods containing around 100 seeds.

A tough tree growing on any soil type, tolerates alkaline soils and limited space. Drought tolerant and reportedly resistant to salt spray and urban pollution. Propagate from seed if available which germinates easily or semi hard wood cuttings.

Terminalia catappa - Indian Almond, Bedam

A large spreading tree with very characteristic horizontal branches making deep shade, under which nothing else will grow. The large leaves, dark green leaves up to 30 cm long, turn copper red and drop at the end of winter but are immediately replaced. The white catkin-like flowers are borne in spring and the edible nuts ripen in late summer.

Does well on well drained sandy soils, salt tolerant and resistant to salt laden winds. The roots are dense and fibrous, good for stabilizing sand but difficult to grow other species under it. Drought and intense summer heat may result in leaf drop, usually replaced rapidly once the temperature moderates. Propagate from seed. Seedlings are sensitive to transplanting and are slow to become established. New leaves are produced all along the length of the trunk. To encourage height rub out the leaf buds on the lower trunk.

Thespesia populnea - Aden Apple, Indian Tulip Tree

Small tree reaching 4-6 m with a similar spread. The dense crown is made up of pretty heart-shaped leaves, giving a dense shady crown. Moderate growth rate approximately 1 m a year. The flower buds are red but when open the flowers are pale yellow with yellow stamens and a dark red base. The flowers look similar to Hibiscus. The fruits are bell-shaped, changing from green to black with maturity.

A hardy tree doing well on poor soils, sandy or limestone. Medium salt tolerance and resistant to salt winds. Requires regular irrigation. Propagate by soft wood cuttings.

Washingtonia - Mexican Fan Palm, Washington Palm

Though vertical growth is relatively slow, approximately 4.5 m in 10 years, the large fan shaped leaves make a considerable spread, even on a three year old tree. The distinctive pleated leaves are very large, 1.5 m across on young trees and even larger on mature trees. There are two very similar species, *Washingtonia filifera* and *Washingtonia robusta*, initially both leaves are covered with string-like threads which die back in *W. robusta* as the leaf matures but persist on *W. filifera*. New leaves are produced from the top while the lower leaves die back giving the straight trunk a skirt of dead leaves which can be trimmed off. Loose white flowers give rise to strings of black fruits, each containing one seed.

High salt tolerance and good drought resistance. Grows well in containers for several years though the plant remains smaller. Like the date palm, even large specimens transplant well. Propagate from seed which germinates easily. Self-sown seedlings are plentiful.

Ziziphus spina-christi - Christ-thorn Tree. **Native**
Arabic name: Sidr

Native to the region, a tree or multi-stemmed bush reaching 10 m. Frequently seen lining the edge of wadi floors. The leaves are small and ovate and the branches erect and thorny. Each leaf has three prominent veins, one in the centre and two running either side, almost parallel. The early spring flowers are green-yellow and though visually insignificant have a pungent sweet fermenting smell which is highly attractive to bees. The fruits look like mini-apples, yellow at first, drying to red-brown. The ratio of edible flesh to stone is variable, irrigated trees have larger fruits. Several other species are cultivated, these have larger leaves and bigger fruits which are sold in local markets.

A tree well suited to regional conditions being drought, highly salt tolerant and able to grow on alkaline soils. Propagate from seed. Soak the seed to rehydrate the flesh then scrape it off from around the stone and wash it clean. Plant the stones half buried as light seems to speed up germination. Germination is variable depending on the condition of the seed. Seed that has been lying on the ground for several months can germinate in as little as 7-10 days at 25-30C. Fresh seed may be very resistant and not easy to germinate immediately, try scarifying the seed with sandpaper before planting or just be patient. The tap root is well developed, use a deep container such as root trainers to allow the roots to develop. Alternatively plant out into the final planting position early when the plant is still small.

Container gardening is very versatile and there is a pot for virtually every space so there's always an opportunity to grow something. Herbs through the winter months, climbers to provide shade or privacy, colourful annuals to cheer up a balcony or paved area.

Which pots

There is a huge choice of both plastic and pottery containers available. Plastic pots are light and versatile but even very good quality ones eventually become brittle in the intense summer sun. They are ideal for temporary planting of winter annuals and then can be washed and stored out of the sun over the summer. Ceramic and pottery pots are more durable and suitable for permanent planting.

Glazed and unglazed pots are made locally and each have their good and bad points. Unglazed pots are lighter and come in a wider variety of shapes but are often relatively fragile. Their porous nature allows water to evaporate from the surface cooling the root zone which is a great advantage in the summer. There is less chance of water logging because excess water can seep out over the entire surface not just out of the drainage holes. Unglazed pots, however, dry out more quickly than glazed ones. Glazed pots are thicker and tougher. Their heaviness is a good counter balance for large plants growing in lightweight peat-based compost. The impermeable pots retain water in the hot months, especially important for permanently planted leafy shrubs. For the same reason, you have to be careful about over-watering plants in glazed pots and the root zone is considerably hotter than in unglazed pots.

Plant Needs

Soil mixes for containers needs to be of high quality with plenty of organic material to act as a reservoir for food and water. Add slow release fertilizer to the original planting mix or regular applications of complete fertilizer for really good looking plants. Use the potting mixes straight from the bag but improve the drainage by adding 10% coarse grained sweet sand or artificial material such as perlite or vemiculite. Pure peat tends to be difficult to re-wet once it has dried out but adding other material helps overcome this problem.

Potting up and aftercare

All pots need good drainage holes and these need to be covered with a layer of gravel or broken pot pieces, to prevent the soil being washed out and holes being clogged up.

Place the new plant in the pot so the original level is a few centimeters below the rim to allow for watering. Tease out the roots and fill around the plant with moistened compost. After planting put the container in a sheltered spot away from heat and wind, or make some temporary shade until the plant becomes established. Water carefully but thoroughly, until the water just begins to run out of the base of the pot. At this point the soil has absorbed all the water it can hold, further watering just washes the nutrients out of the soil. Ensure the pot is thoroughly watered and then let it partly dry out before watering it again.

Watering multiple pots can be a time consuming task. There are multiple ways of setting up some sort of automatic watering system. Add big pots to the irrigation system by threading fine tube onto the drippers. Mini independent irrigation systems are available which can water up to 12 pots from a water reservoir. Individual watering spikes can be attached to soft drinks bottles to provide a constant water supply. Capillary matting is also useful to provide pot plants with steady moisture. Self watering pots are also available where there is a reservoir section below the pot and the moisture is wicked up to the roots.

Pot maintenance

Plants need re-potting when their roots start growing through the drainage holes. Prepare a new pot, the next size up, as above.

Top Dressing

Plants which have grown too big to re-pot can be given a new lease of life by top dressing. Carefully remove the top 2-5 cm of compost and replace it with fresh material mixed with slow release fertilizer.

Re-potting in the same pot

By pruning back both the roots and branches a plant can be re-potted with new compost in the same pot. Prepare the plant by watering well the night before and pruning the branches. Take the plant out of the pot and stand it on the original upturned pot. Work over the root ball teasing out the roots and removing the old compost until the entire root ball is reduced by 5 cm all round. Now re-pot the plant with new compost and keep it sheltered for a few days while it gets reestablished.

Narrower necked pots make it is impossible to remove the plant without destroying it. As an alternative consider breaking open the base of the pot and burying it slightly in open ground, continue to feed and water. The roots will quickly grow through the pot base and the plant will continue to flourish.

Which plants

Small annuals and annual climbers

Alyssum maritimum	Sweet Alyssum
Celosia species	Cockscomb and Plumed
Coleus blumei	Coleus
Gazania splendens	Gazania
Gomphrena globosa	Globe Amaranth
Impatiens walleriana	Busy Lizzie
Ipomoea alba	Moon Flower
Ipomoea tricolor	Morning Glory
Ipomoea quamiclit	Cyprus Vine
Pelargonium (zonal)	Geraniums
Petunia species	Grandiflora and Multiflora
Portulaca grandiflora	Sun Plant
Salvia splendens	Red Sage
Tagetes	Small Marigolds

Medium sized annuals and perennials

Adenium	Desert Rose
Asystasia gangetica	Asystasia
Catharanthus roseus	Vinca
Carissa grandiflora	Natal Plum
Clitoria ternatea	Blue Pea Flower
Hibiscus rosa-sinensis	Hibiscus
Ixora coccinea	Ixora dwarf forms
Lantana camara nanna	Dwarf Lantana
Plumeria	Frangipani
Plumbago capensis	Cape Plumbago

Large perennial shrubs and climbers

Antigonon leptopus	Coral Vine.
Bougainvillea	Bougainvillea
Ficus benjamina	Weeping Fig
Jacquemontia pentantha	Jacquemontia
Jasminum	Jasmine, Spanish or Common
Nerium oleander	Oleander
Pennisetum setaceum	Fountain Grass green or red
Plumeria	Frangipani
Quisqualis indica	Rangoon Creeper double flower
Washingtonia	Californian Fan Palm

Autumn; September to December

As temperatures decrease in autumn plants come alive. Many trees such as *Cassia fistula* and *Millingtonia* and climbing vines *Quisqualis,* Rangoon Creeper and *Campsis*, Orange Trumpet Vine, produce a second show of flowers. The majority of shrubs e.g. *Hibiscus, Caesalpinia*, Peacock Flower, *Jatropha* and *Bougainvillea*, really come into their own during this period.

Feeding

Actively growing plants require feeding. Complete fertilizer and slow release products are good for annuals and shrubs but relatively expensive. For large areas and trees agricultural pelleted fertilizer can be watered in. Try high phosphorus (K) fertilizer to encourage flowering. Loosen the soil round shrubs, dig in compost and animal manure and water well. Plant new shrubs and trees just at the beginning of the active growth period.

Cuttings

Once plants are growing well take cuttings, as this is the best time of year. Cuttings taken in autumn have enough time to establish before the cooler weather comes and are large enough by the summer to withstand the summer heat.

Seeds

Start sowing seeds, choose the most robust first as autumn can still have bursts of high heat which can destroy delicate seedlings; *Tagetes, Zinnia*, and *Ipomoea tricolor,* Morning Glory, are all in this category. Check if night time temperatures are consistently below 30°C before planting the majority. Plant seeds in several batches, this will give a much longer flowering period and as an insurance against failure. Try germinating tree seeds especially of native species which are hard to find in nurseries.

Insects

Insects and pests re-emerge; treat at the first signs of activity before the really active season begins.

Winter; late December to February

Brief periods of cold or salt laden wind can defoliate plants. Move pot plants to a sheltered site and consider sheltering prize plants with shade net or suitably placed garden furniture. Winter storms are often brief and protecting plants for 24 hours can save several weeks of flowers.

Some trees and shrubs become dormant, stop feeding and reduce watering. Generally reduce irrigation systems to a minimum.

Continue to germinate seeds for spring and early summer flowering. Some plants require cooler temperatures to germinate, 15-18°C being ideal for *Gazania*. Germinate *Zinnia, Catharanthus, Petunia* and *Gaillardia* which will now flower well into the summer.

Spring; February to May

As the day length increases and temperatures begin to rise, plants start to make rapid new growth. This is the main flowering period for trees with dramatic displays such as *Cassia fistula*, Indian Laburnum, *Peltophorum*, Yellow Flame Tree and the native species *Ziziphus*, *Prosopis cineraria* and *Moringa peregrina*.

Annuals
This is the best time for many annuals such as Geranium as the increasing daylight length stimulates them to flower. Others may now look rather long and straggly (Petunia and Alyssum), trim them back to 15 cm and feed and water well for a new lease of life. Once the night time temperature rises to over 30°C bring in Geranium and *Impatiens*, Busy Lizzie, and 'over summer' as house plants where they will continue to flower. Sow seeds of tough annuals for summer flowers. Zinnia; the large single bloom types do well but do not last as long as the smaller bushy types such as 'Profusion'. Others to consider are *Celosia*, Cockscomb, and *Tagetes*, Marigold. Basil germinated now will survive the summer given a shady place.

Cuttings
Cuttings taken now root quickly, but will probably need shade protection over the summer. It is best to delay planting them out into the open garden until autumn, apart from really hardy plants such as *Catharanthus*, Vinca, and *Portulaca*.

Summer; May/June to September

Annuals
The hot season really begins in earnest at the end of April and by May most winter annuals will have withered and died. Remove spent annuals and cut off water supply to annual and herb beds. Compost all the debris; high heat accelerates the composting process. Empty plastic containers, clean and store out of direct sunlight to prolong their life. Use the spent compost to improve the soil in the garden. *Portulaca* cuttings can be taken all summer and will rapidly flower. Try germinating Zinnia, Vinca and Marigold seeds in the early part of the summer.

Containers
Soil in containers can heat up as much as 30% above the air temperature so if the air temperature is 37°C the soil in the container could be up to 50°C. Try to protect container plants as much as possible by grouping them together under partial shade to create a micro-climate of cooler conditions.

Shrubs and Trees
For many plants this is a dormant period with little or no growth. By mid-summer even *Hibiscus* and *Bougainvillea* have slowed down. Prune back shrubs and trees to reduce water consumption. Plants which flourish during the summer are particularly valuable such as *Campsis*, Orange Trumpet Vine. It often doesn't even start new growth until May, by June and July it is in full flower and growing vigorously. Layer stems to create new plants.

Irrigation
This is the period of maximum water consumption. Try to conserve water as much as possible by watering at night when loss through evaporation is at its lowest. On humid days in coastal areas watering can be reduced. If green algae starts to grow on the surface the garden is being over watered or the drainage may need to be improved. Shade new plants which wilt by midday with inexpensive beach umbrellas.

KEY REGIONAL PLANT NURSERIES

Like many shops in the Middle East the plant nurseries are often grouped together in one area, though of course there are individual shops scattered throughout the region. Tools and irrigation equipment are often stocked separately and many supermarkets and DIY stores also stock some gardening products.

Abu Dhabi – Nursery location: Al Meena district north west of the city
Take Meena Street and continue on until it becomes 20th Street, past the City Police Station. At the next roundabout turn left and at the T junction turn left. There are 20-25 small shops in this area, some with A/C interiors for house plants, others with exterior shade netting. Stock includes a full range of plants, plus potting compost, fertilizers and pots. GPS 24°30'59.66"N, 54°22'29.66E

Dubai – Nursery location: Eastern edge of the city beyond Wassan 2
From Ras Al Khor take Route 44 towards International City. After passing it on the right take the next turning to the right on to Route 54. The Municipality Nursery (marked on Google Maps) is on the left. The approximately 20 large private nurseries are in a block behind the Municipality Nursery and are clearly visible. They were relocated from the Garhoud Bridge area in 2008-2009. Dubai nurseries stock a full range of plants, including a wide range of imported plants. They also stock potting compost, fertilizers and pots. GPS 25°09'08.89"N, 55°27'30.09E

Oman - Nursery location: Near As Seeb village
From Muscat International Airport take the main highway towards Sohar and take the turn off sign posted As Seeb. Turn onto Al Shimalya St. at the roundabout and go straight across to A'raudhah St. The 15 or so large nurseries are on both sides of A'raudhah St. plus some on Way 344. The nurseries stock a wide variety of plants, fertilizers, sand and wadi soils, potting compost, pots, some tools and irrigation equipment. Many of the nurseries grow their own plants. GPS 23°39'43.41"N, 58°11'55.85"E

Sharjah – Nursery location; Al Jubail district by the fruit and vegetable market
Head towards the Heritage District on Corniche St., after it crosses Al Arouba St., you pass the Sharjah Fruit and Vegetable market on the right hand side. Beyond this are 15-20 individual shops selling a range of plants, potting composts, fertilizers, pots, some tools and sweet sand. GPS25°21'06.84"N, 55°22'47.22"E

SALINITY TOLERANCE TABLE

Plant Name	ppm	Plant Name	ppm
Drinking water	1,500		
Sea Water	35,000	Ipomoea pes-caprae	6,500
Albizia lebbeck	6,000	Ixora coccinea	1,000
Allamanda	1,000	Jacquemontia pentantha	1,000
Alternanthera versicolor	2,500	Jasminum officinale	2,000
Antigonon leptopus	1,750	Jatropha integerrima	2,500
Atriplex species	10,000	Lantana species	3,000
Azardirachta indica	2,000	Leucaena leuccephala	8,000
Bauhinia purpurea	1,000	Moringa oleifera	4,200
Bougainvillea species	2,000	Moringa peregrina	4,500
Caesalpinial gilliesli	5,500	Nerium oleander	9,000
Caesalpinial pulcherrima	4,000	Parkinsonia aculeata	9,000
Callistemon species	2,500	Peltophorum pterocarpum	3,000
Campsis	1,750	Phoenix dactylifera	20,000
Carissa macrocarpa	2,500	Pithecellobium dulce	5,000
Carpobratus edulis	4,500	Plumbago auriculata	1,500
Cassia fistula	1,500	Plumeria species	3,200
Casuarina equisetifolia	9,500	Pongamia glabra	1,000
Catharanthus roseus	4,000	Prosopis cineraria	4,500
Clerodendron inerne	8,000	Prosopis juliflora	30,000
Clitoria ternatea	3,500	Quisqualis indica	1,500
Conocarpus lancifolius	7,000	Tecoma species	4,200
Cordia sebestena	4,100	Terminalia catappa	4,500
Ficus religiosa	4,500	Thespesia populnea	6,000
Ficus microcarpa	6,000	Thevetia peruviana	7,000
Ficus benjamina	3,500	Thumbergia erecta	1,200
Gazania	2,000	Vitex agnus-castus	6,500
Hibiscus rosa-sinensis	2,000	Washingtonia filifera	20,000
Ipomoea batatas	4,000	Wedahlia trilobata	2,500
Ipomoea palmata	2,000	Ziziphus spina-christi	9,000

Websites & Other Sources

Emirates Natural History Group www.enhg.org/
Flowering Trees of the World www.flickr.com/groups/beautifulfloweringtreesoftheworld
Global Invasive Species Database www.issg.org/database/welcome/
Oman Botanic Garden www.oman-botanic-garden.org
Royal Botanic Gardens Kew Database http://epic.kew.org/datasources.htm
Thompson and Morgan Seeds www.thompson-morgan.com
Top Tropicals http://toptropicals.com/
UAE Interact http://www.uaeinteract.com/
UBC Botanical Garden and Centre for Plant Research www.ubcbotanicalgarden.org
United States Department of Agriculture www.usda.gov/wps/portal/usda/usdahome
University of Florida 680 Tree Fact Sheets http://hort.ufl.edu/trees/
USDA Natural Resources Conservation Service http://plants.usda.gov/

Selected Bibliography

Brown, D. The royal Horticultural Society New Encyclopedia of Herbs. Dorling Kindersley 2002.
Brickell, C. The Royal Horticultural Society encyclopedia of gardening. Dorling Kindersley 1992.
Brickell, C. The Royal Horticultural Society gardeners' encyclopedia of plants and flowers. Dorling Kindersley Ltd. 1989
Courtright, G. Tropica. Timber Press 1992
Kwei, T. Landscape Plants in the U.A.E. T. Kwei, New York. 1978
Love, A. Gardening in Oman and the Gulf. Apex Publishing. 1995
Mandaville J. P. Jr. Wild Flowers of Northern Oman. Bartholomew Books, 1978.
Marley, E & Kay, S. Gardening in the Gulf . E. Marley, Dubai 1990.
Miller A. G. & Morris M. Plants of Dhofar. The Office of The Advisor for Conservation of the Environment, Diwan of Royal Court Sultanate of Oman.
Moore, E. Gardening in the Middle East. Stacey Int. 1986
Phillips, R. & Rix, M. Conservatory and Indoor Plants Vol 1 & 2 Pan Books 1998
Pickering, H. & Patzelt, A. Wild plants of Oman. Royal Botanic Gardens Kew 2008
Toogood, A. The Royal Horticultural Society Propagating Plants. Dorling Kindersley 1999.
Winbow, C. The Native plants of Oman, The Environmental Society of Oman 2008

COMMON NAME INDEX

Scientific Name	Common Name
Ficus microcarpa	Chinese Banyan
Asystasia gangetica	Chinese Violet
Allium schoenoprasum	Chives
Ziziphus	Christ-Thorn Tree
Celosia	Cockscomb
Coleus blumei	Coleus
Antigonon leptopus	Coral Vine
Coriandrum	Coriander
Wedelia trilobata	Creeping Daisy
Ipomoea quamoclit	Cyprus Vine
Phoenix dactylifera	Date Palm
Ruellia tweediana	Desert Petunia
Adenium	Desert Rose
Moringa oleifera	Drumstick Tree
Caesalpinia pulcherrima	Dwarf Poinciana
Delonix regia	Flame of the Forest
Ageratum houstonianum	Floss Flower
Nicotiana	Flowering Tobacco
Pennisetum setaceum	Fountain Grass
Plumeria	Frangipani
Boswellia sacra	Frankincense
Pelargonium	Geranium
Calotropis procera	Giant Milkweed
Gomphrena globosa	Globe Amaranth
Duranta erecta	Golden Dewdrop
Coreopsis tinctoria	Golden Tickseed
Allamanda cathartica	Golden Trumpet Vine
Hibiscus rosa-sinensis	Hibiscus
See page 46	Ice Plant
Terminalia catappa	Indian Almond
Cassia fistula	Indian Laburnum
Ixora coccinea	Ixora
Jasminum	Jasmine
Jatropha integerrima	Jatropha
Parkinsonia aculeata	Jerusalem Thorn
Amaranthus tricolor	Joseph's Coat
Dombeya elegans	Kenyan Wedding Flower
Thunbergia erecta	Kings Mantle
Conocarpus lancifolius	Kuwaiti Tree
Ficus microcarpa nitida	Laurel Fig
Pithecellobium dulce	Manila Tamarind
Calendula officinalis	Marigold
Tagetes	Marigolds
Washingtonia	Mexican Fan Palm
Chrysanthemum paludosum	Mini Marguerite
Mentha	Mint
Ipomoea alba	Moon Vine
Ipomoea tricolor	Morning Glory
Rhoeo spathacea	Moses-in-the-cradle
Murraya paniculata	Murraya
Carissa grandiflora	Natal Plum
Azadirachta indica	Neem
Nerium oleander	Oleander
Campsis grandiflora	Orange Trumpet Flower
Origanum	Oregano
Tradescantia spathacea	Oyster Plant
Alternanthera versicolor	Parrot Leaf
Petroselinum crispum	Parsley
Tabebuia	Pink Trumpet Tree
Tabernaemontana divaricata	Pinwheel Bush
Pongamia glabra	Pongamia
Acacia nilotica	Prickly Acacia
Tradescantia pallida	Purple Heart
Bauhinia purpurea	Purple Orchid Tree
Allamanda violacea	Purple Trumpet Vine
Ipomoea palmata	Railway Creeper
Albizia lebbeck	Rain Tree
Quisqualis indica	Rangoon Creeper
Ficus religiosa	Sacred Bo
Salvia officinalis	Sage
Cordia Sebestena	Scarlet Cordia
Sesuvium portulacastrum	Shoreline or Sea Purslane
Lantana camara	Shrub Verbena
Antirrhinum	Snapdragon
Leucaena leucocephala	Speedy Tree
Ipomoea batatas	Sweet Potato
Leucophyllum frutescens	Texas Sage
Prosopis juliflora	Thorn Tree
Lantana montevidensis	Trailing Lantana
Millingtonia hortensis	Tree Jasmine
Nyctanthes arbor-tristis	Tree of Sorrow
Catharanthus roseus	Vinca
Ficus benjamina	Weeping Fig
Urechites lutea	Wild Allamanda
Clerodendrum inerme	Wild Jasmine
Cassia siamea	Yellow Cassia
Peltophorum pterocarpum	Yellow Flame Tree
Thevetia peruviana	Yellow Oleander
Tecoma stans	Yellow Trumpet Flower

INDEX

12